Retire Right

The Practical Guide to RRIFs, Annuities and Pensions

KIRK POLSON & GEORGE BRETT

ft

Penguin Books

PENGUIN BOOKS
Published by the Penguin Group
Penguin Books Canada Ltd., 10 Alcorn Avenue, Suite 300, Toronto, Canada, M4V 3B2
Penguin Books Ltd., 27 Wrights Lane, London W8 5TZ, England
Viking Penguin Inc., 40 West 23rd Street, New York, New York 10010, USA
Penguin Books Australia Ltd., Ringwood, Victoria, Australia
Penguin Books (NZ) Ltd., 182-190 Wairau Road, Auckland 10, New Zealand
Penguin Books Ltd., Registered Offices: Harmondsworth, Middlesex, England
Published in Penguin Books, 1994
10 9 8 7 6 5 4 3 2 1

Canadian Cataloguing in Publication Data
The National Library of Canada has catalogued this publication as follows:
Polson, Kirk, 1950 –
    Retire right
(Financial times personal finance library)
Annual.
At head of title: Financial times.
Following title: The practical guide to RRIFs, annuities and pensions.
Description based on: 1992.
ISSN 1193-896X
ISBN 0-14-024377-1 (6th ed.)
1. Retirement income – Canada – Planning – Periodicals. 2. Retirees – Canada – Finance,
Personal – Periodicals. I. Brett, George, 1938-1992. II. Title. III. Title: Financial times.
IV. Series.

HG179.P64   332.024'01   C93-030682-1

Cover design: Creative Network
Cover illustration: Peter Yundt

The information contained in this book is intended only as a general guide and may not be
suitable for certain individuals. If expert advice is warranted, readers are urged to consult a
competent professional. While the investment, legal, tax and accounting information contained in this book has been obtained from sources believed to be accurate, constant
changes in the legal and financial environment make it imperative that readers confirm this
information before making financial decisions.

CONTENTS

Tables and Illustrations

Introduction

WELCOME TO THIS, OUR 6TH edition of *Retire Right*. As we look back at the two governing federal political parties in Canada since our first edition in 1988, the Progressive Conservatives under Brian Mulroney and most recently the Liberals under Jean Chretien, there has been a common message in all budgets: Canadians must shoulder more responsibility for their own retirement. The social security system that has been built since World War II is not going to be expanded further. In fact, it is likely that deficit-conscious governments will, if anything, continue to chip away at programs already in place for retired Canadians.

The erosion of government benefits started a number of years ago when Michael Wilson, then minister of finance, announced the "claw back" of Old Age Security benefits for those individuals with a net income in excess of $50,000. The February 1994 budget brought down by the Liberals introduced another "claw back" — this time of the age credit currently available to Canadians aged 65 and over. Sweeping changes to registered retirement savings plan (RRSP) contribution limits were rumoured prior to budget day 1994, but the government chose to announce that a comprehensive review of our retirement system would take place over the next year.

Against this backdrop of changing government benefits, retired Canadians have had to deal with uncertainty in the financial markets. Interest rates declined from a high of 12 percent to as low as 4 percent by February 1994, only to rise to 8 percent just four months later. The Toronto Stock Exchange which had soared in 1994, bounced around during the first half of 1994 causing many who had hoped to escape low interest rates by hopping aboard the mutual fund bandwagon to jump right back off by mid-1994.

Inflation, that bee in the bonnet of those living on fixed incomes, dropped to below 2 percent during this period of lower interest rates, compared to 6 percent or 7 percent a few years back. As real rates of return remain higher, some might argue that retired Canadians are better off. Try telling this to retirees who are consumers of services, which have risen in cost faster than the rate of inflation.

Along with these economic uncertainties has been the death of more financial institutions. Canadians now have to look beyond a promised rate of return to the long-term viability of an institution. Questions about how to best operate and fund the Canada Deposit Insurance Corporation and the life insurance industry's consumer protection plan, CompCorp, have surfaced. Financial institutions are changing; more and more mergers and acquisitions are taking place as companies try to compete profitably in the global economy.

Over the years we have been given a firmer grip on our personal retirement savings through increases in the foreign content allowed for RRSPs, the flexibility of the registered retirement income fund (RRIF) and, more recently, new options such as the life income fund (LIF) for locked-in pension monies.

All this activity is going on against a changing demographic backdrop. According to a Statistics Canada report on future population trends, seven million Canadians will be sixty-five or older by 2031. That's almost three times as many as now. The number of young is expected to decline almost as dramatically. Some 6.2 million Canadians are now under seventeen, but by 2031 this number is expected to shrink to four million. Actuary Robert Brown of the University of Waterloo, wrote in the preface to his 1991 book, *Economic Security in an Aging Population*: "At present, Canada has one of the youngest populations in the Western world, as measured by the percentage of the population aged sixty-five plus to those aged twenty to sixty-four. By the year 2030 (only forty years hence) we will have one of the oldest populations."

Quite simply, there will be fewer working-age Canadians to support those who have retired when those born during the baby boom of the late 1940s and 1950s start collecting Old Age Security. So our governments are right: we must take more responsibility for our own retirement security.

Recognizing the reality of the situation, the government has moved to make it easier to put together the retirement dollars we will need. It has begun to phase-in planned increases in the annual contribution limits for RRSPs as part of a comprehensive rewriting of the rule book for tax-supported retirement savings.

Although earlier federal pension standards reform, and similar legislation in Ontario, applies only to contributions starting in 1987, these reforms are a great improvement over the legal minimum requirement on contributions before 1987. In the case of these contributions, an employee must be at least forty-five years of age and have ten years of service with his employer before he has access to employer contributions.

There have been other changes that will make pensions more portable between employers. While Ottawa did not go agree to a homemakers' pension, women pensioners have been put on an equal footing with men. It is now mandatory under federal law for employers who offer pensions to give a surviving spouse a continuing pension of at least 60 percent of the employee's pension. And surviving spouses in most cases must receive the full value of the pension earned by an employee who dies before retirement.

The reforms aimed at improving women's pensions are vital for two reasons. A woman working full-time in Canada earns 62 percent of what her male counterpart makes, so she starts with a major handicap. On top of that, she is likely to live longer.

However, regardless of whether you are a man or a woman, the new reality is that the government has presented you with an unassembled retirement kit and provided the tools to put it together. You should consider *Retire Right* your set of assembly instructions. It provides an easy-to-understand explanation of the government security blanket, employer pensions and retirement income options.

It might help to think of these three aspects of retirement financing as a stool that is most stable with equal support from all three legs. If you don't have an employer pension – whether because you're self-employed or because your employer doesn't offer one – the do-it-yourself retirement income must do the work of two legs to keep the stool upright.

As important as it is to build steadily for retirement, most retirement guides skimp on the flip side – getting out of RRSPs when the time comes to buy RRIFs, annuities or other products that provide monthly income in retirement. *Retire Right* will act as your source of information when it comes time to consider retirement options.

About the authors

Kirk Polson, of the Polson Financial Group retirement income specialists in Toronto, makes a living finding retirement solutions for people converting their RRSPs into monthly income. He is a graduate of York University in Toronto, a chartered life underwriter, a chartered financial planner and a chartered financial consultant. Mr. Polson has also contributed to the *Financial Times of Canada*. George Brett was a *Toronto Star* business reporter who started the newspaper's Dollars & Sense column in 1981 and regularly answered questions on retirement topics. He also wrote *The Star*'s annual in-depth income tax section. He died in April 1992.

Acknowledgments

The authors thank the following people for their invaluable assistance in the preparation of this book:

Yvan Clermont and Charles Larocque, Employment and Immigration Canada, Hull.

Peter Hobday, Income Security Programs, Human Resources Development Canada.

Allan Kirkland, retired senior systems analyst, *The Toronto Star*.

Minnie Lawrence, chartered accountant, Markham, Ontario

Ian Markham, a partner in Peat Marwick Thorne Actuarial and Benefits Inc., Toronto.

Bill Solomon, a partner in GBB Buck Consultants Limited, Toronto.

Alex Melvin, president of CANNEX, a company that provides independent surveys of the rates offered by Canadian financial institutions.

Sita Ramdial of Polson Financial Group, who helped compile the statistics for the tables.

Jim Rogers, principal in The Rogers Group in Vancouver and a retirement income specialist, who over the years has generously given of his time and shared concepts of benefit to retired Canadians.

Thanks are also due to Susan Polson who is truly "the wind beneath my wings." And to Cara, Terri and Derek Polson, whose endless energy and *joie de vivre* are an inspiration every day.

Kirk Polson
September 1994

CHAPTER 1

A Budget for the Long Term

IF YOU'RE LIKE MOST PEOPLE, setting up a household budget may be the last thing you want to do. But if you've ever gone through this tedious exercise, you've probably found it rewarding. It enables you to know, rather than guess, the state of your personal finances.

You might have discovered, for instance, that you have trouble paying your monthly bills because your spending exceeds your income. Remember Charles Dickens' lines from *David Copperfield*: "Annual income twenty pounds, annual expenditure nineteen nineteen six, result happiness. Annual income twenty pounds, annual expenditure twenty pounds ought and six, result misery."

The truth might hurt a little. But when you know the sobering facts, you can convert your misery into happiness by cutting your spending, increasing your income or doing both. It's perfectly simple, even if it is more easily said than done.

That's why *Retire Right* was conceived – to help you prepare a retirement income plan and budget. We want you to enjoy Dickensian happiness, not just now but for the rest of your life.

Our concern is not with getting your income and spending to balance next month, but in five, ten or thirty years from now. As with household budgeting, you can bring your retirement spending into line with your retirement income. Our emphasis will be on ways you can beef up your income in retirement. And the more time you have until you retire, the better your chances of success.

Still, retirement budgeting, like household budgeting, must be realistic. You'll be able to work out what you can and can't afford, and if necessary trim your expectations as well as increase your income. This realism is vital because you can't risk outliving your income.

Just as in household budgeting, there are concepts and terms to learn in retirement budgeting. Yes, they're more complicated than their domestic counterparts, but our job is to demystify them for you.

Retire Right is for those of you who are faced with decisions about what to do with your RRSP, what company pension options to choose and how to use your cash savings to produce the income you'll need when you retire. *Retire Right* is also for those of you who have already retired or are nearing age seventy-one. By the end of the year in which you turn seventy-one the law requires that you wind down your RRSP. And it's for those of you with a long-term perspective who look down the road when you're in your thirties and forties and realize that retirement income planning is a serious business in an era of permanent inflation.

If you're wealthy, you won't need this book. But if you're an average Canadian, you're going to have to make some critical decisions as you approach retirement, or in the early years of your retirement – decisions that involve major sums of money. You won't have adequate retirement income if you rely entirely on government pensions, and your employer pension might not do the job either.

Why should you plan your retirement now? So you can adapt your spending to fit your lifestyle, rather than being forced to curtail your travelling and other retirement activities because your income is inadequate. Whether you have managed to save $25,000 or $500,000 for your retirement, we'd like to help you avoid mistakes.

How much will you need?

Woody Allen said: "Money is better than poverty, if only for financial reasons." It's funny, but true. Tomorrow's retirement income depends on decisions you made years ago as well as RRIF, annuity and pension choices you'll make today. A wrong decision can affect you, your spouse and what you leave behind after your death.

How much will you need? One of the biggest concerns of people over fifty years of age is whether they'll have enough money after retirement. It is sometimes suggested that when people retire, they'll need to start with 65 percent to 75 percent of pre-retirement income, although what you need and what your neighbour needs might differ substantially.

Take the real-life example of a university professor who regularly travelled, played tennis and enjoyed scuba diving during the Christmas holidays, spring breaks and summer holidays. Although it might be easy to guess what kind of activities she was likely to

Your Annual Expenses

WHERE YOUR MONEY GOES	NOW	IN RETIREMENT
Living expenses		
Rent or mortgage		
Property taxes		
Property insurance		
Repairs and maintenance		
Electricity		
Water		
Heat		
Telephone		
Food		
Clothing		
Entertainment		
Clubs		
Sports		
Vacation		
Transportation		
Gas & oil		
Insurance		
Maintenance		
Public transportation		
Health Care		
Health insurance premiums		
Employer health plan		
Medicine		
Dental care		
Pension/RRSP contributions		
CPP/QPP contributions		
Life insurance premiums		
Income taxes		
UIC premiums		
Other		
Loan repayment		
Gifts and donations		
Miscellaneous		
TOTAL ANNUAL EXPENSES		

enjoy during retirement, she has discovered that her reduced income does not allow her to participate in her favourite activities to the same extent. On the other hand, there is the example of a retired insurance company manager who spends nine months of the year with his wife at their cottage. This couple lives quite comfortably on 60 percent of his pre-retirement income.

So far we have hardly mentioned inflation. Even at a 4 percent inflation rate, the value of money is reduced by half in eighteen years. At 6 percent it's reduced by half in twelve years; at 8 percent money loses half its value in nine years.

What should you do? Clearly, if we could all give retirement a dry run before we had to do it for real, we would see how well it was working, both financially and in terms of using our time. But most of us can't, so a few words of advice are in order:

• If you are getting close to retirement, review your spending habits. Assume you'll need 70 percent to 75 percent of your pre-retirement income to retire when you want to, not when you have to.

• Start keeping track of what you spend, right down to the newspaper you buy on the way to work and the quarter you put into a parking meter. Yes, it's a tedious exercise. But it's the only way to get a handle on what you're doing with your money.

• If you're close to retirement, or even going to retire this year, complete Worksheet I. List what you spend now. Adjust for items that will drop off after retirement, such as commuting to work, and for expenses that will increase, especially leisure activities.

If you take these steps, you should have a good feel for what you would need if you retired today.

CHAPTER 2

Will You Have Enough?

A MAN ATTENDING A RETIRE-
ment seminar once got up and said he wanted to enjoy his money
"during my mobility, not my senility." And while it's difficult to
argue with his sentiment, it doesn't eliminate the necessity of long-
term planning when you're winding down your RRSP – unless, of
course, your health is poor.

If you retire at age sixty, which many people are doing these
days, you could have more than a third of your lifetime ahead of
you. When you were twenty-five you might have believed that anyone over fifty was "ancient," but when you're sixty and hearing
about RRIFs and annuities that run until age ninety, you might
laugh nervously.

Statistics developed by insurance companies show that men aged
sixty-five may live another eleven to fifteen years, depending on
whether they smoke. Women the same age who smoke have a life
expectancy of seventy-nine, while non-smoking women may live to
age eighty-four. (You can look at Statistics Canada's estimates of life
expectancy in Chart I.) So you can see how a decision at age sixty-
five to take all the money out of your RRSP or RRIF over ten years
could backfire if you outlived your plan. On the other hand, holding
everything for a rainy day assumes you'll live until that rainy day.

What is needed is a realistic appraisal of how long you want your
income to last. For life? Until you and your spouse have both died?
Age eighty-five? Age ninety-five? It's a tough decision, since you
can't know when you'll die. But don't jump to conclusions about
how long you'll need income or how much you'll need. Your annual requirements may taper off substantially after age seventy-five,
when most people slow down. On the other hand, inflation may
send costs skyrocketing. A loaf of bread, for instance, may cost $5
within fifteen years.

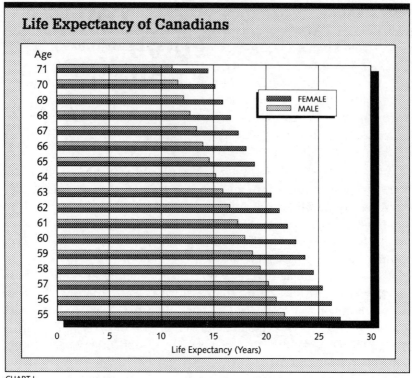

CHART I

A strident protest erupted in 1985 when the Progressive Conservative government threatened to partly de-index Old Age Security (OAS), the "universal" government pension. However, the government quickly changed its mind when confronted with an unprecedented show of "Gray Power."

If nothing else, the revolt against removal of inflation protection drove home the point that pensioners are the one group of Canadians who understand the difficulties of living on a fixed income.

Most retired people have no inflation indexing in their income except for OAS and Canada Pension Plan (CPP) retirement benefits.

Unfortunately, that indexing doesn't go far in meeting the growing expenses of retirement. However, as you'll see later, there are steps you can take upon winding down your RRSP to combat inflation. Just how much of a problem inflation presents is largely dependent on your lifestyle. But when coupled with the reduction in income experienced by most people at retirement, it can present a serious obstacle.

For example, if you retired twelve years ago in Toronto, you've seen inflation erode your income by an average of 6 percent to 7 percent a year. The compound effects of inflation mean the purchasing power of your money has been reduced by half. If you retired with a $1,000-a-month unindexed pension twelve years ago, its purchasing power today would be just $500. With the same inflation rate, it will be worth only $250 in another twelve years.

You must also consider your after-tax position. Suppose you are a pensioner who invests in Canada Savings Bonds with a 6 percent interest rate. If you are in a 27 percent tax bracket, your after-tax earnings on the bonds will be 4.4 percent – barely enough to keep pace with inflation in some areas of Canada, unless it maintains the 2 percent level of 1993 and 1994.

People aged sixty-five to seventy-five find it particularly hard to cope on a fixed pension that offers no built-in inflation protection. They're active and they want to enjoy travel and other expensive, inflation-prone activities. Those seventy-five to eighty-five are usually affected less dramatically in terms of purchasing power because

The Effect of 4% Inflation on Your Purchasing Power

Your Income Today	10 Years from Today	20 Years from Today
$ 18,000	$ 26,644	$ 39,440
20,000	29,605	43,823
24,000	35,526	52,587
30,000	44,407	65,744
36,000	53,299	78,880
40,000	59,210	87,645
48,000	71,051	105,174
50,000	74,012	109,556
60,000	88,815	131,468
75,000	111,018	164,334
100,000	148,024	219,112

TABLE I

How Many Years Will Your Money Last?

		Rate of Return on Your Investments				
		5%	6%	8%	10%	12%
Annual	6%	37				
Rate of	8%	20	24			
Withdrawal	9%	17	19	29	Years	
	10%	14	16	21		
	12%	11	12	14	19	
	15%	8	9	10	12	14

TABLE II

they often cut down on expensive leisure activities. Those who run into increased medical costs or the need for nursing-home care are the exceptions.

Table I shows how much income you'll need in ten to twenty years, with a 4 percent annual inflation rate. A ten- to twenty-year period is appropriate, based on the life expectancies shown in Chart I.

Sobering numbers? Don't despair. In later chapters we'll show you how to arrange your financial affairs to protect you from inflation. For now, you must determine whether you are saving enough. Worksheets II and III and their accompanying tables at the end of this chapter will help provide a quick estimate of your future nest egg and the annual income it will produce, whether you're twenty years away from retirement or five years away. But be conservative in your assumptions; it's better to err on the safe side.

If you're about to retire and you haven't saved enough, you'll have to cut back on spending. Alternatively, you might be able to postpone your retirement for a year or two or take a part-time job. If you still have a few years to go, you know how much you should save in coming years to meet your goals. To help you make your appraisal, use Table II to determine how long your money will last, assuming you take out a specific sum each year at given interest rates.

For example, let's say you have $100,000 in savings that is earning 10 percent. You wish to withdraw $12,000 a year. Simply find the point on the table where your withdrawal rate ($12,000 or 12 percent of your savings) meets your expected rate of return, 10 percent. You'll find your money will last nineteen years. By also referring to the life expectancy table, you can determine whether your rate of withdrawal is reasonable. For a man age sixty-five, life expectancy is 14.57 years, so in our example there is sufficient capital to last to life expectancy if our investor earns 8 percent to 10 percent on his money.

If you're married, you'll also have to give careful consideration to how much your spouse will need in the event of your death. You may have a company pension plan that provides for continued payments to your spouse if you die first but typically, such payments are reduced by as much as 40 percent. As a result, your spouse would have to make do on less income than the two of you were receiving when you retired. This amount may be reasonable today, but ten years from now the surviving spouse may need every dollar of the original pension.

Sources of Retirement Income

	Husband	Wife
Pensions		
Employer pension		
CPP/QPP		
Old Age Security		
Guaranteed Income Supplement		
Spouse's Allowance		
Government annuity		
Foreign pension		
RRSP annuity		
RRIF		
Investment Income		
Interest		
Dividends		
Capital gains		
Prescribed (i.e., non-RRSP) annuity		
Rental Income		
Property #1		
Property #2		
Property #3		
Business Income		
Employment Income		
Other Income		
Total (a)		
Estimated income tax (b)		
Disposable income (a − b)		
Family disposable income		

WORKSHEET II

We'll go into detail about this aspect of retirement income planning later, but for now it would be wise to add up how much income will be available to you and your spouse when you retire.

Setting Your Retirement Objectives

YOUR RETIREMENT INCOME NEEDS

A. My present annual income (before taxes) is $_____

B. If I retired tomorrow I would need an annual income in today's dollars of (assume 65% to 85% of A above) $_____

C. I intend to retire in_____years at age_____

D. When I retire I will require income for _____ years. (Refer to life expectancy table. Be conservative.)

E. During retirement I expect my assets will earn a return of _____ %

WHAT YOU HAVE ACCOMPLISHED TO DATE

F. My estimated annual CPP/QPP benefits $_____

G. My estimated annual Old Age Security benefits $_____

H. My estimated pension from my employer (use for defined-benefit-type pension only) $_____

I. Other pensions available to me $_____

J. Therefore, my estimated annual pension benefits are (F + G + H + I) $_____

K. Amount of annual income I will still require in today's dollars (B - J) $_____

MAKING UP THE DIFFERENCE

L. At retirement my annual income shortage will be (K times expected inflation factor in Table IV for number of years until retirement) $_____

M. When I retire I will need the following capital to make up the annual income needed in L above (L times expected rate of return factor for number of years income will be required. See Table III.) $_____

N. Sources of capital available to me at retirement:
RRSP $_____

Company pension (money purchase) $_____

Assets to be liquidated (e.g., business, home) $_____

Inheritances $_____

Other sources of capital $_____

Total $_____

O. Amount of savings I still require (M–N) $_____

P. Therefore, I need to save the following amount each year (Line O divided by the factor in Table V) $_____

WORKSHEET III

Retirement Income Factors

Years* I Will Need Income	Expected Rate of Return on Capital		
	6%	9%	12%
10	7.802	6.995	6.328
11	8.360	7.418	6.650
12	8.887	7.805	6.938
13	9.384	8.161	7.194
14	9.853	8.487	7.424
15	10.295	8.786	7.628
16	10.712	9.061	7.811
17	11.106	9.313	7.974
18	11.477	9.544	8.120
19	11.828	9.756	8.250
20	12.158	9.950	8.366
21	12.470	10.129	8.469
22	12.764	10.292	8.562
23	13.042	10.442	8.645
24	13.303	10.580	8.718
25	13.550	10.707	8.784
26	13.783	10.823	8.843
27	14.003	10.929	8.896
28	14.211	11.027	8.943
29	14.406	11.116	8.984
30	14.591	11.198	9.022
31	14.765	11.274	9.055
32	14.929	11.343	9.085
33	15.084	11.406	9.112
34	15.230	11.464	9.135
35	15.368	11.518	9.157
40	15.949	11.726	9.233

*Review the life expectancy table and add or subtract a number of years to reflect your health and family longevity.

TABLE III

Inflation Factors

Years Until I Retire	Annual Rate of Inflation		
	4%	6%	10%
1	1.040	1.060	1.100
2	1.082	1.124	1.210
3	1.125	1.191	1.331
4	1.170	1.263	1.464
5	1.217	1.338	1.611
6	1.265	1.419	1.772
7	1.316	1.504	1.949
8	1.369	1.594	2.144
9	1.423	1.689	2.358
10	1.480	1.791	2.594
15	1.801	2.397	4.177
20	2.191	3.207	6.727
25	2.666	4.292	10.835
30	3.243	5.743	17.449
35	3.946	7.686	28.102
40	4.801	10.286	45.259

TABLE IV

Investment Return Factors

Years Until I Retire	While I am Saving, My Capital Will Earn		
	6%	10%	14%
5	5.975	6.716	7.536
10	13.972	17.531	22.045
15	24.673	34.950	49.980
20	38.993	63.002	103.768
25	58.156	108.182	207.333
30	83.802	180.943	406.737
35	118.121	298.127	790.673
40	164.048	486.852	1529.909

TABLE V

CHAPTER 3

Your Retirement Income House

THERE'S NO DOUBT THAT choosing pension, RRIF and annuity options can be a complex task. But these days, what financial matter isn't?

There are ways to make the job simpler. If you work methodically and seek qualified advice, you'll be in a better position to make the choices that will suit your needs. Above all, give yourself plenty of time. Start looking and asking well before you're forced to make a choice at age seventy-one. We recommend approaching your retirement income needs as if you were building a house. The foundation of this house will be government benefits: CPP or Quebec Pension Plan retirement payments and OAS (unless you are required to pay back OAS benefits under the "clawback" affecting those individuals whose net income is in the $53,000 plus range).

If you're retiring today and need $40,000 a year to live on, you know that the government-built foundation provides almost $13,000 a year ($12,986.16 in the third quarter of 1994 if you qualify for maximum benefits), and both pensions are fully indexed to compensate for inflation. The trick is to build as much inflation protection as you can for the remaining three-quarters of your retirement income.

For many people, the main storey of the retirement house is an employer pension. This pension, coupled with OAS and CPP/QPP benefits, may provide the guaranteed income base needed to meet everyday living expenses. If, as in our example, your employer pension is $28,000 a year, you've met your $40,000 requirement.

But what about the majority of Canadians who don't have pensions? If you are without a pension, or have an inadequate one, consider using an annuity or a conservative, guaranteed RRIF or LIF for this storey of your retirement income house. RRSP funds can be used to buy an annuity or RRIF that will produce enough income to

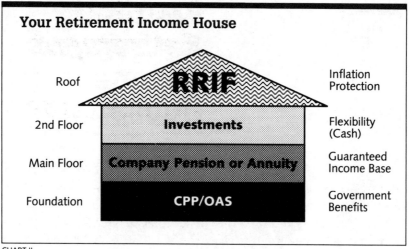

Your Retirement Income House

Roof	RRIF	Inflation Protection
2nd Floor	Investments	Flexibility (Cash)
Main Floor	Company Pension or Annuity	Guaranteed Income Base
Foundation	CPP/OAS	Government Benefits

CHART II

meet your day to day needs. (The income from a RRIF could fluc-
tuate if not guaranteed for the life of the plan.)

Once you've managed to build the foundation and main storey,
you'll have the guaranteed income base you need. Then you can go
about building a second storey, which should consist of easily redeemable investments to meet sudden cash requirements. Think of
the second storey as the one that allows flexibility. Let's say you
want a new car or decide to take a major trip. Where's the cash to
come from? For most people, liquid investments are the best source
of dollars for major non-recurring expenses.

A roof over your head

Then, of course, you need a roof over your retirement income
house: long-term protection against inflation, with some built-in
flexibility. What better use for the RRIF. Consider what you accomplish with this house approach:
  • You build a guaranteed base of income through government
  benefits, a company pension or LIF and an annuity or RRIF.
  • There is built-in flexibility in the form of cash investments,
  such as Canada Savings Bonds, treasury bills and stocks.
  • You put some or all of your RRSPs into a RRIF to augment your
  basic guaranteed income.
And then you sit back and enjoy your retirement.

CHAPTER 4

Keeping Retirement In Perspective

SAVING FOR RETIREMENT IS hard work that demands sacrifices now to provide financial security in your senior years.

If you're young and have recently landed your first full-time job, there's too much in life that demands urgent attention without thinking seriously about your income needs in forty years. And if you're young and have recently married, your long-term financial priorities will likely include a home, an education for the kids and non-retirement investments that might someday buy a cottage or an around-the-world trip.

There's nothing wrong with these priorities. In fact, the usual rule of thumb – that you have at least three months' salary in the bank before you embark on an investment program – will rule out even non-retirement investing for most young people. For many, it's hard enough to scrape together enough for food, rent and clothing. And those with employer pension plans – even if they aren't great plans – can count themselves among the lucky ones. (Even they should not be lulled into a false sense of security. They should be saving on their own; who knows where they or their companies will be in 10 or 20 years.)

Keep in mind, however, that things are going to improve. By the time your family has grown, chances are your home will be largely paid for, you'll be buying a new car every three or four years and you'll be reading the financial pages of your newspaper to find the best investments.

So if you're young, there's no pressing need to put retirement planning on your priority list. Just plan to put it there when you can – but before it's too late. And that means thinking seriously about RRSPs, the tax-sheltered savings that you can convert at retirement into monthly income cheques to supplement your government and employer pensions.

RRSPs allow your retirement savings to grow much more quickly than they would in a non-sheltered environment. Thanks to the magic of compounding, the growth of the interest you earn year after year can be astounding. If you contributed $2,000 a year for thirty years to an RRSP that earned 8 percent interest for the entire time, you'd have $226,000.

Unfortunately, you may not have the money to make contributions today. And while the federal government has moved to increase allowable RRSP contributions to as much as $15,500 a year, rising limits mean little if you can't scrape up a dollar to put toward your retirement.

But there is more good news. The government is also going to let you carry forward unused RRSP contributions for up to seven years, or more in some cases. That could be a boon when, years from now, you have money to spare but are lamenting the lost years when you couldn't make contributions.

Think about it. And plan for it.

CHAPTER 5

Old Age Security and Supplements

HOW MUCH DO YOU NEED TO contribute to your RRSPs to produce adequate retirement income? You can't even begin to answer the question until you know how much you'll get from the government and, if you belong to a pension plan, from your employer.

Both the government pension plans – OAS and the CPP – are discussed in detail in this section of *Retire Right,* while employer pensions are the subject of Part III. First, let's look at OAS, government income supplements, taxation and some other benefits before moving on to the CPP.

And by the way, none of these benefits comes automatically. You have to apply for them, and you'll lose money if you don't apply in time.

Old Age Security

OAS is the "universal" government pension most Canadians receive starting at age sixty-five. Eligibility depends primarily on length of residence in Canada, so even most non-working spouses qualify. You get it even if you keep working beyond age sixty-five, but no matter when you collect, the payments are taxable.

Today, 3.3 million people receive OAS benefits. Of these, nearly 40% have sufficiently low incomes to qualify for a federal supplement, known as the Guaranteed Income Supplement (GIS). There are also provincial income supplements, as well as three versions of the federal Spouse's Allowance.

You normally apply only once to receive OAS for life. Application forms are available from the Income Security Programs offices of Human Resources Development Canada (listed in the blue Government of Canada pages at the back of your telephone directory). To be on the safe side, it's a good idea to apply six months before you turn sixty-five.

OAS remains fully indexed; that is, Canadians will continue to receive quarterly increases covering any rise in the Consumer Price Index following the decision by the Brian Mulroney government to abandon its original proposal to make pensioners absorb the first 3 percent of inflation each year.

OAS began in January 1952 as a $40-a-month pension for people aged seventy and over. Starting in 1965, the age threshold was reduced year by year until the present eligibility age of sixty-five was established. In the third quarter of 1994, the full OAS payment was $387.74 a month.

Guaranteed income supplement

Once you're approved for OAS, you will be sent a separate form used to determine whether your income is low enough to make you eligible for the GIS.

GIS and other income-dependent benefits are paid on a sliding scale that reduces entitlement by about $1 for each $25 of yearly income, or $50 for a couple. In the third quarter of 1994, this supplement – which originated in 1967 – amounted to a maximum of $460.79 a month for a single pensioner of sixty-five or over and $300.14 for a married pensioner.

Because the level of GIS payments depends on the recipient's income, which can vary, you must reapply every year. Unlike OAS, GIS payments are not taxed. OAS and GIS monthly payments are combined in one cheque.

Provincial supplements

Six provinces and the two territories provide benefits for pensioners to supplement federal OAS and GIS payments. Nova Scotia, Ontario, Manitoba, Saskatchewan, Alberta, British Columbia, the Northwest Territories and the Yukon Territory provide these top-up benefits.

The programs differ in a number of ways, including the amount of payments provided. Most provide monthly payments to GIS recipients only, and these are paid separately from the federal OAS/GIS cheque. Like GIS payments, they are non-taxable. The provincial and territorial income supplement programs are listed, with addresses and phone numbers, in the appendix of this book, Where to Get More Information.

Spousal benefits

When one spouse has turned sixty-five and qualifies for the GIS, and the other is between sixty and sixty-five and meets income and residence requirements, the younger spouse is entitled to Spouse's Allowance – a maximum of $537.81 a month in the third quarter of 1994. That's the same as OAS, plus half the maximum GIS at the married rate. Spouse's Allowance – which began in 1975 – really amounts to receiving OAS and GIS payments early. It is not taxable and is paid only while both spouses are alive.

There are other spousal benefits as well: Extended Spouse's Allowance and Widowed Spouse's Allowance. Both paid a maximum of $759.42 a month in the third quarter of 1994.

Extended Spouse's Allowance, introduced in 1979, allows for a continuation of payments to a person sixty to sixty-five upon the death of a spouse. Widowed Spouse's Allowance is directed primarily at older women, a chronically low-income group, and carries the same residence, income and age requirements. This benefit, introduced in September 1985, goes beyond Spouse's Allowance and Extended Spouse's Allowance in that it does not require either the recipient or the recipient's spouse to have previously qualified for income-dependent benefits. To qualify for Widowed Spouse's Allowance, an applicant must have been legally married to a partner who has died, or have lived for at least a year with a common-law spouse who is deceased. Neither the spouse's age at death nor the date of death is a factor. However, eligible applicants must not have remarried.

Annual applications are necessary for Spouse's Allowance. Application forms are available from Income Security Programs offices of Human Resources Development Canada. All three varieties of the allowance may, in certain circumstances, be paid retroactively for up to a year.

Spouse's Allowances are currently paid to more than 112,000 Canadians between the ages of sixty and sixty-five. However, single or divorced people cannot qualify for any form of Spouse's Allowance, and some people think this is discriminatory. Three people have challenged the legislation under the Charter of Rights, and at the time this book was written, this was still before the courts.

If you leave the country, Spouse's Allowance and all other income-dependent benefits are paid for the month of departure and six more months, then suspended. The benefits will be resumed on your return if you still qualify, although missed benefits cannot be recovered.

Tax credits

Starting with the 1988 tax return, personal tax exemptions and some deductions have been converted to credits. The reason is fairness: credits are worth the same to everyone, while exemptions give greater tax savings to those earning more money. Under the old system, exemptions reduced taxable income; under the new one, credits reduce tax. The credits are non-refundable, meaning that if you don't owe tax, any unused portion of credits won't result in a refund. (Refundable credits, such as the child tax benefit, are exceptions.)

For seniors, the most important credits are the pension credit and age credit. The pension credit of $170 ($200 in Quebec) reduces tax on employer pension income (but not on OAS or CPP/QPP benefits) at any age and on annuity and RRIF income starting at age sixty-five. At one time the age credit could be regarded as a gift which you received from the government each year once you reached age sixty-five. However, the 1994 federal budget changed that. Now the age credit results in a tax reduction of up to $950 a year, a benefit which is reduced by income over $25,921. It is completely eliminated once your net income reaches $49,100. This change will be phased in over 1994 and 1995; only half of the credit will be "clawed back" in 1994, all of it in 1995.

Because of the way provincial income taxes are tacked onto federal taxes, the credits are worth more than their nominal value. If we look at the pension income credit, the $170 is the equivalent of the basic federal tax on the first $1,000 of taxable income. In addition, you save the federal surtax and provincial tax on the $1,000.

Both credits are transferable between spouses. If your spouse lacks the income to use his or her pension and age credits fully, you may use the unused portions to reduce your taxes. That's in addition to your own credits.

What about people born outside Canada?

Partial OAS pensions are available to some people who haven't lived in Canada long enough to qualify for the full pension.

Until July 1, 1977, there were no partial pensions. You received either the full OAS or nothing. The general eligibility period was forty years' residence in Canada after age eighteen. This meant, for example, that if you had been born in Canada and lived here all your life, you could leave the country at fifty-eight and still start receiving OAS at age sixty-five anywhere in the world.

A more generous option under the old rules permitted the pension to go to a person who had only ten years of legal residence in Canada immediately before application. In other words, someone could immigrate as late as age fifty-five and still get full OAS benefits at sixty-five. If Canadian residence during the ten years preceding application was interrupted, three years' prior presence (not necessarily permanent residence) in Canada for each year elsewhere were required in order to be eligible for benefits. Under this option, a person also had to be resident in Canada for a full year immediately preceding approval of the application.

Obviously, there were inequities. Under these rules, for example, someone who had lived in Canada for thirty-nine years after turning eighteen but who had left before turning sixty-four would get no OAS benefits.

But under new rules introduced in 1977, a person beginning Canadian residence on or after July 1 of that year earns 1/40th percent of the OAS for each year of residence in Canada after age eighteen. So the person in our example above would receive 39/40ths percent of the full pension.

There is an important caveat: unless Canada has a social security agreement with the person's previous country, at least ten years of residence in Canada is needed before the minimum pension of one-quarter of the full OAS is allowed. In Table VI, you can see the status of Canada's agreements as of July 1991.

You'll notice that Canada has no social security agreement with the United Kingdom. If you're British-born, we suggest you contact the British Pensioners Association (Canada), listed in the appendix, Where to Get More Information.

People who became residents of Canada before July 1, 1977 can choose to qualify under either set of rules, but most will be better off under the old ones. For instance, a person who came to Canada in January 1970 at age fifty-eight needed to wait only until January 1980 – after ten years' residence – to qualify for the full pension starting in February 1980 at age sixty-eight. However, a person who came to Canada in January 1982 at age fifty-eight would qualify only for 10/40ths of the full OAS benefits in February 1992 after ten years of residence.

There is also "the twenty-year rule," which stipulates that you must have lived at least twenty years in Canada after age eighteen to take OAS outside the country and continue receiving it indefinitely. Residence in Canada after you have started receiving the benefit counts as part of the twenty-year total. Otherwise, you will receive the pension for the month you leave and for six months after that. It will then be suspended, but will be reinstated on application after your return – if you still qualify.

If you've lived in Canada all or most of your life, receiving OAS is simply a matter of sending a completed application form to your local Income Security Programs office of Human Resources Development Canada. But for people born in other countries, the application process is not as simple unless you are from the European Commonwealth countries or the United States.

Liberalizing the system

Are you ready for more complications? They may make matters difficult, but you'll welcome them if they result in a larger pension.

The OAS/GIS system was liberalized in 1984. The most important change, known as the topping-up provision, relates to how OAS and GIS work together.

If you're awarded a partial OAS, that's what you'll get for life. If it's a half pension at age sixty-five, you will still receive half the current OAS maximum if you live to 100. But while OAS will grow only to keep pace with inflation, the 1984 changes allow a potentially large increase in the GIS for immigrants of limited income.

Suppose someone has come from another country and, at age sixty-five, has fifteen years' residence in Canada. We'll assume the period of residence was interrupted and the person can't qualify for the full pension immediately. If he wants to take OAS now, it will be only 15/40ths of the full amount.

Under previous legislation, he would have received 37.5 percent of OAS plus the maximum GIS in the absence of other income. As a result of 1984 changes, he receives enough additional GIS payments

Canada's Social Security Agreements

Agreements in force

Antigua and Barbuda	Australia	Austria
Barbados	Belgium	Cyprus
Denmark	Dominica	Finland
France	Germany	Greece
Iceland	Ireland	Italy
Jamaica	Jersey/Guernsey	Luxembourg
Malta	Netherlands	Norway
Portugal	Saint Kitts-Nevis	Saint Lucia
Spain	Sweden	United States

Agreements Signed (not yet in force)

Switzerland

Agreements under negotiation

Mexico	Morocco	New Zealand
Phillippines	Trinidad and Tobago	

SOURCE: HUMAN RESOURCES DEVELOPMENT CANADA

TABLE VI

so that total OAS and GIS payments will be the same as the full OAS plus maximum GIS. In other words, the federal government is providing a full pension for a person lacking any other income, even though he or she doesn't qualify under the residency rules.

Another 1984 change extended the period of back payments of OAS for an eligible person who did not apply for it in time from one year to five years.

Finally, if someone dies who was entitled to OAS and/or GIS but had not applied for them, the estate, an heir or a legal representative can apply within a year of death and receive the money posthumously – up to five years of OAS and one year of the GIS. The original legislation did not allow posthumous applications.

CHAPTER 6

The Canada Pension Plan

THE OTHER MAJOR CANADIAN government pension, in addition to OAS, is the Canada Pension Plan, which covers people in all parts of Canada except those eligible for the Quebec Pension Plan (QPP).

The CPP dovetails with OAS to provide basic income security in retirement. It also pays benefits to the families of deceased contributors and to severely disabled contributors and their children. While OAS is a non-contributory pension based on years of residence in Canada, CPP pensions are financed by mandatory contributions made through payroll deductions or, in the case of the self-employed, through direct payments to Revenue Canada. Contributions start at age eighteen for those employed at that age.

CPP benefits, whether they result from retirement or are triggered by death or disability, are almost always proportional to contributions. This relationship between contributions and benefits means that the average CPP retirement benefit in 1967, the first year of payouts, was only $19.97. This was because CPP contributions had begun only in January 1966. People still receiving those early pensions have not received an increase, except for inflation adjustments.

While OAS is adjusted quarterly to keep pace with inflation, CPP inflation adjustments are made only in January, based on the previous year's inflation.

Employees contributing to the CPP did so at a rate of 1.8 percent of "maximum pensionable earnings" from 1966 through 1986. While the 1.8 percent did not change in those twenty years, the maximum pensionable earnings figure increased each year to keep pace with inflation, and still does. In 1994 it was $34,400. Your employer also paid 2.6 percent or, if you were self-employed, you paid the entire 5.2 percent.

Beginning in 1992, the government embarked on a policy of increasing contributions for twenty-five years. It is scheduled to peak at 10.10 percent in 2016. The increase, which was initiated to ensure that the CPP remains financially secure, is 0.2 percent a year until 1996, 0.25 percent for 1997 to 2006, and 0.20 percent for 2007 to 2116. For people earning the maximum pensionable earnings or more, annual CPP contributions in 1994 were $806 for an employee (plus an equal amount from the employer) and $1,612 for a self-employed person.

Collecting early

Another major change in the CPP also went into effect in 1987. You can now choose to retire and stop paying into the CPP and start collecting retirement benefits as early as age sixty or as late as age seventy. This differs from past practice, when benefits began at sixty-five, with one exception: a contributor still working beyond this age who had not qualified for maximum benefits could continue contributions until age seventy or until he or she had qualified for maximum benefits, whichever comes first.

Whether retirement benefits are taken early or late, there is an adjustment in the amount payable of 0.5 percent a month or 6 percent a year. Therefore, a person who starts receiving benefits at age sixty gets 30 percent less to start than the person who starts at sixty-five, and the person who hangs in until seventy gets 30 percent more. This flexible retirement policy, adopted first by the QPP, requires that you have "substantially" quit working at the time you apply for benefits.

The most you could make from employment in 1994 and still qualify for early CPP retirement benefits was $8,333. When you apply for early benefits, you have to estimate your earnings for the next twelve months, rather than for the calendar year. Strangely enough, once you've qualified, you could return to work without affecting your CPP benefits. In no case can you make contributions after you start receiving your benefits.

The following is a summary of CPP benefits paid in 1994. Keep in mind that the figures shown are maximums, and there are many instances where people receive less because they have not been in the plan since the beginning and/or because their income was not high enough for them to contribute at the maximum rate:

• The age-sixty-five retirement benefit maximum in 1994 was $694.44 a month.

• Although the disability pension had been $455.64 a month in 1986, a change in the calculation formula resulted in a jump to $634.09 in 1987. In 1994 it was $839.09. For a person to qualify, the disability must be "severe and prolonged," and of such a serious nature that the person is unable "to pursue gainful employment" of any sort. Unlike the disability benefits paid by provincial workers' compensation boards, the CPP disability pension is never a partial one. Either you qualify or you don't. But as mentioned above, benefits will vary according to the amount of contributions and how long they have been made.

• A lump-sum death benefit – the 1994 maximum is $3,440 – is paid to the estate of a deceased contributor.

• A surviving spouse thirty-five or over receives a CPP survivor's pension. For a person between forty-five and sixty-four, the 1994 maximum is $384.59 a month. It's $416.66 if the person has turned sixty-five. Spouses between thirty-five and forty-five at the time of the contributor's death have their benefits reduced unless they have a "severe and prolonged" disability (and can't work) or have dependent children. Although survivors' benefits were cut off at remarriage up to the end of 1986, they now continue. If your survivor's benefits ended because of remarriage, you can apply to have them reinstated.

• When a CPP contributor dies or begins receiving CPP disability benefits, his or her child gets flat-rate benefits – $160.47 a month in 1994 – that continue until age eighteen, or up to age twenty-five if attending school full-time. These children's benefits are an exception to the rule that benefits are based on contributions. Since 1987, a child who has lost the earning power of both CPP-contributing parents through disability or death has been allowed to claim two children's benefits. A further change allows the benefits to continue after the child's marriage.

Splitting credits

Another change made in 1987 affected the division of CPP credits. Human Resources Development Canada previously split CPP credits upon application after divorce or legal annulment. The credits for the period of cohabitation of both former spouses were simply added together and divided by two, subject to some exclusions. The ex-spouses must have lived together for at least thirty-six consecutive months during their marriage with the divorce taking place after January 1, 1978. The application had to be made within three years after the divorce became final. A written agreement could stop the splitting of the CPP credits.

Effective in 1987, a division of credits is mandatory upon divorce or annulment, unless there is a written agreement between the former spouses that is valid under a provincial law which explicitly states that there will not be a division of CPP credits. (Only Saskatchewan and Quebec have such laws.) After a year of separation beginning in or after 1987, a legal or common-law spouse can apply to have the credits split. A written agreement can still stop the splitting of CPP credits.

In a continuing marriage or common-law union, a spouse who is age sixty or older may apply to have CPP pension income split. By putting more income into the hands of the lower-income spouse, this arrangement may result in lower overall tax. Upon the death of the first spouse, the survivor reverts to individual entitlement.

There is also the child-rearing dropout provision. It is designed to protect individuals who suffer a loss or reduction of earnings as a result of child care responsibilities. It should be noted that a full-time homemaker who has never contributed to the CPP is still entitled to OAS at age sixty-five, but not to CPP retirement benefits, except in the case of credit-splitting resulting from divorce or separation.

The dropout clause

The CPP also features a little-known advantage for contributors called the 15 percent dropout clause. It's not an additional benefit, but a generous way of calculating contributions. The dropout clause allows years of low contributions – even none in some circumstances – without reducing benefits.

While the general rule is that you contribute to the CPP from age eighteen to sixty-five, you get a break if you enter the work force late (if you're going to university or can't find a job), if you are unemployed for an extended period or if you take a sabbatical outside the country. The dropout period is calculated automatically by computer, which searches for 15 percent of the lowest monthly contributions during the person's working life and excludes them.

This means CPP retirement benefits are based on the other 85 percent. But if you're contributing at the maximum rate, it also means you can fail to make contributions for 15 percent of your working life in circumstances such as the above without suffering a penalty. In fact, if you have been contributing to the CPP all your life, you can retire and stop contributing at a certain age – currently sixty-one – then begin receiving the same benefits at sixty-five as you would if you had contributed up until the previous month. However, as long as you're working in Canada, you can't simply choose to stop making CPP payments at age sixty-two. To find out how long you would be able to "drop out" from making CPP contributions at your age, get in touch with your local Income Security Programs office.

You should also contact the office for information on how to apply for CPP benefits. They don't come automatically, and in some cases are retroactive for only a year.

The Quebec Pension Plan

The QPP began at the same time as the CPP and was essentially identical. It employed the same contribution basis of 3.6 percent of maximum pensionable earnings and an identical inflation adjustment. The step-up in contributions since 1987 is also at the same rate and the Quebec plan pays the same amounts as the CPP in most instances.

The key difference is not in collecting or paying out contributions, but in how funds are invested. CPP funds are used as a pool of ready cash from which nine of the ten provinces borrow, while QPP contributions flow into Quebec's pension investment fund, the Caisse de dépôt et placement du Québec.

Over the years, however, other differences have evolved. The QPP preceded the CPP in allowing a person to begin receiving retirement benefits at any time between ages sixty and seventy. A second difference between the two plans lies in the maximum pensions paid to surviving spouses of contributors. At some ages, payments are greater under the QPP. On the other hand, the flat-rate benefits paid to children of people receiving disability benefits and to orphans of contributors are higher under the CPP.

Finally, there is a difference in eligibility rules for a person receiving disability benefits. Under either plan, the general rule is that the disability must be so severe that the person is unable "to pursue gainful employment" of any sort. But while the CPP continues this stiff test to age sixty-five, when retirement benefits kick in, the QPP relaxes the rule at age sixty. To qualify for disability benefits starting at this age, you need only have "a total incapacity to fulfill the requirements of your last job."

In addition to being the equivalent of the CPP for Quebec residents, the QPP regulates employer pensions, a function performed in other provinces by pension commissions.

CHAPTER 7

Are You Entitled to a Foreign Pension?

IF YOU IMMIGRATED TO Canada some years ago and you are now nearing retirement, you may be entitled to both OAS and a pension from your country of origin. That's quite apart from your eligibility for CPP retirement benefits, which are based on mandatory contributions through employment or self-employment.

In addition, if you come from a country with which Canada has a social security agreement, Canadian and foreign pension eligibility can be based on the combined years of residence or contributory credits in Canada and the country of origin. This means you may qualify for a pension, or a higher pension, despite limited Canadian residence. It may also enable you to export your pension if you have fewer than twenty years of Canadian residence.

Inquire now

If you think you might be eligible, inquire right away. You won't get a foreign pension without applying for it. And with the bureaucracies of two countries to deal with, you'll likely need plenty of time, patience and persistance.

There are a number of places to go for information. One is the Ottawa embassy or high commission of the country from which you hail. Another is the nearest consulate of that country.

But the best might be your local Income Security Programs office of Health and Welfare Canada. Look under "H" in the blue Government of Canada pages at the back of your telephone directory. How Health and Welfare handles your inquiry will depend on which of three categories your country of origin falls under.

The first category is countries with which Canada has social security agreements. (Table VI in Chapter 5 details the status of Canada's social security agreements with other countries.) Your Income Security Programs office may have the necessary forms, information on qualifying requirements and a list of documents the country requires as proof of eligibility.

When you complete the appropriate forms, they will be sent to Health and Welfare's Office of International Operations in Ottawa. If the proper forms are not available locally, you will be asked to fill out an interim application for foreign benefits. It will then be sent to the Office of International Operations, which will send you the specific form that applies to your country of origin. Complete it and send it to the Ottawa office.

Applications are processed according to the provisions of the particular social security agreement, then forwarded to the foreign pension authority. If necessary, Health and Welfare will include a statement of your contributions to the CPP and your years of residence in Canada.

The second category includes countries with which Canada has initiated negotiations on a social security agreement, or with which it has signed an agreement that is not yet in force. Included here are the Republic of Ireland, Switzerland, Trinidad and Tobago, and Yugoslavia. In the case of these countries, you will be asked to fill out an interim application, but it will be held until the agreement comes into force.

With the third group – countries that have no social security agreement with Canada and no immediate prospect of one – your Health and Welfare office can only direct you to the embassy, high commission or consulate. It may also provide you with the address of the appropriate social security office of the country concerned so you can write for information. This group includes the United Kingdom and Eastern Bloc countries.

Don't give up
If you come from one of the countries in this third group, don't be dissuaded from inquiring even if there is no immediate prospect of a social security agreement. In the case of the United Kingdom in particular, there is a well-established procedure for finding out about and applying for pensions. (There are addresses listed in the appendix, Where to Get More Information.) It's just that in the absence of a social security agreement, you have to do most of the work yourself.

CHAPTER 8

A Look at Pension Reform

IN THE WORLD OF PENSIONS, 1981 was a landmark year. That's when the foundations of the coming pension reform era were built at a national pension conference in Ottawa attended by pension industry professionals and senior representatives of the federal and provincial governments.

For many years it had been apparent that employer pensions – the corporate and government pensions now provided to about 37 percent of working Canadians or 4.6 million people – were inadequate. The main problem was that pension standards legislation, where it existed, specified that you had to be at least forty-five years of age and have ten years' service with an employer before you were entitled to the employer's pension contributions. Unless your employer offered a better deal, this meant only your contributions, plus interest, were refunded when you left your job. And if your pension plan was non-contributory, you got nothing. As a result, you could work all your life for five or six employers, all having pension plans, without ever becoming entitled to a cent of an employer's money.

The 1981 meeting changed all this. The federal government and the province of Ontario (which between them have more than one-third of pension members) have since passed legislation requiring, among other things, that vesting of pensions take place much sooner. Most other provinces have also updated their pension laws.

The remaining provinces clearly need to bring in or amend pension standards legislation. But are legislative safeguards adequate in jurisdictions that brought in reforms during the 1980s?

With the important exception of inflation indexing, the subject of the next chapter, the answer is yes.

Laurence Coward, director emeritus of benefits consulting firm William M. Mercer Ltd. and an authority on pensions, puts the matter in perspective. "The poorest people in Canada are no longer senior citizens," he says. "They're single parents and the unemployed who have used up their Unemployment Insurance credits."

Elderly Canadians who are entitled to Spouse's Allowance, OAS and the GIS have the sharp edge of poverty slightly dulled. But Mr. Coward says that for people earning minimum wages, "It would be a waste if they had to contribute to pensions. They'll be better off in retirement with the government benefits."

Federal and Ontario reforms

Let's take a look at the federal and Ontario pension reforms, then move on to what other provinces have done.

The federal legislation, known as the Pension Benefits Standards Act, covers all employees and employers under federal jurisdiction. Crown agencies, banks, broadcasting, communications, shipping, trucking and a hodgepodge of other sectors fall into this category. The act also covers anyone working in the Yukon and Northwest Territories.

Ontario's Pension Benefits Act governs people in Ontario who belong to pension plans, except those covered by the federal law. Here are the key features of the federal and Ontario laws:

• Vesting – the point at which you get the right to your employer's contributions – takes place after two years of plan membership. The pension contributions are also locked in (meaning you can't get cash out) at this point. The new vesting and locking-in rules apply only to pension money accrued – that is, contributions and earnings on the contributions – starting in 1987. The "45-and-10" rule still applies to pre-1987 accruals unless the plan sponsor has agreed to apply the current vesting rules to all service.

• If you leave your job to go to another, you now have extensive portability rights if the federal and Ontario laws apply. You have the option of transferring the value of your pension credits to a locked-in RRSP (unlike the usual RRSP, you can't withdraw money and the plan is used to buy a life annuity at retirement); to your new employer's pension (although the new employer doesn't have to allow this, and most don't); or to a deferred annuity that would begin paying at your normal retirement age. You can also leave the money with your old employer so you will have a deferred pension at retirement.

• To counter criticism that surviving spouses in the past often had no pension rights, the required form of a pension for a married employee is joint-and-survivor, with the survivor entitled to at least 60 percent of the full pension that the married retiree was receiving. This provision applies to the entire pension, not just to benefits accrued starting in 1987. By signing a waiver form, couples may opt out of this provision or elect a lower survivor pension. The result will be higher monthly pensions. It is only reasonable to opt out if your spouse is adequately protected by his or her own personal wealth, adequate retirement income from another source or by an insurance policy.

• The employer must finance at least 50 percent of the pension on accruals from 1987 on. This provision addresses an inequity under the old legislation that allowed employers to avoid making contributions for an employee who left before "45-and-10."

• Every employee with two years' service must be allowed to join the employer's pension plan. Membership is not compulsory under the legislation, although it may be under the terms of a particular plan. The right to join a pension applies also to part-time employees with either twenty-four consecutive months of service earning at least 35 percent of "maximum pensionable earnings" – the earnings level at which maximum CPP contributions are made ($34,400 in 1994), or 700 hours of employment. It is permissible to have one pension plan for most employees and a more generous one for management.

• Women used to get lower pensions than men in the same jobs because on average they live longer and the benefit is likely to be paid longer. But unisex rates apply on pension accruals starting in 1987, and some employers are voluntarily extending the principle to pre-1987 accruals. There is a downside, however. When a defined-benefit pension (the type to which most pension plan members belong) is commuted because a woman leaves her job, the unisex provision results in her receiving less on pension accruals since the start of 1987 than under the previous sex-distinct rates.

• When an employee dies before receiving a pension, the surviving spouse is entitled to 100 percent of the pension accrual from 1987 on. Otherwise, the estate gets an equivalent lump sum.

• Employees are entitled to retire up to ten years before the usual retirement date of sixty-five – even against an employer's wishes

– and still get pensions based on their vested contributions. Payments in this case are reduced to reflect the lesser contributions inherent in the person's shortened working life and the fact that the payments will be made for a longer time.

Ontario is unique in having an employer-financed fund, the Pension Benefits Guarantee Fund, to make up shortfalls if a company fails without leaving enough money in the pension kitty. There are limitations, however. The guarantee fund does not apply to pension plans less than three years old or to benefits created less than three years before the plan is wound up. Nor does it apply to any part of a pension exceeding $1,000 a month.

The other provinces

Alberta: Portability options here are similar to those of the federal government and Ontario and eligibility is virtually identical. Employers must make at least half of total pension contributions as of 1987. Vesting of pension accruals in 1987 or later occurs after five years with the "45-and-10" rule applying to previous accruals. At least 60 percent of the pension's value from 1987 on must be paid to the surviving spouse, when the employee dies after retirement.

British Columbia: B.C. passed its first pension benefits act, based closely on Alberta's, in June 1991. Some provisions were effective in 1991 but it will not take full effect until January 1, 1993,

Manitoba: Employers must provide at least 50 percent of pension financing as of 1985. Full-time employees must join pensions after two years of service. Five-year vesting and locking in apply to pension accruals in 1985 or later. Two-year vesting and locking in of accruals apply if still a member of the plan in 1990. Otherwise, accruals start in 1990. Previous benefits are subject to the "45-and-10" rule for locking-in and ten years service for vesting.

New Brunswick: Pension standards rules are in force as of December 31, 1991. They provide for pension plan membership after two years of employment, and require vesting and locking-in after five years. The plan may stipulate the maximum employee cost, which can be greater than 50 percent. However, if the plan is silent on this point, the employer must contribute at least 50 percent. Under the legislation, at least 60 percent of the pension's value from January 1, 1992 on is to go to the surviving spouse if the employee dies before retirement.

Newfoundland: Starting with 1985 accruals, the "45-and-10" rule applies to vesting and locking in, with no province-wide standard for benefits earned previously. There are no standards for portability, survivor benefits or minimum employer contributions.

Nova Scotia: Employees are eligible for pension plan membership after two years. Vesting and locking in take place after two years for pension accruals as of 1988. Portability rules are the same as the Ontario and federal provisions. Nova Scotia also requires employers to contribute at least half of pension financing. The 60 percent rule applies to survivor benefits whether the employee dies before or after retirement.

Prince Edward Island: P.E.I. passed its first pension benefits act in April 1990. The targeted proclamation date is January 1, 1993, with the legislation effective one year later. It is modelled on the Nova Scotia and Ontario legislation.

Quebec: The Quebec Supplemental Pension Plans Act was passed in 1989 and most provisions went into effect on Jan. 1, 1990. Its features include survivor benefits of at least 60 percent, the recognition of common-law relationships for death benefits if both spouses were unmarried, generous portability privileges, the right to a reduced early-retirement pension as early as age fifty-five and two-year vesting on accruals starting in 1990.

Saskatchewan: Vesting and locking-in of pension accruals prior to January, 1994 take place after one year of pension plan membership if the employee's age and years of service add up to at least forty-five. For accruals from January 1, 1994 vesting and locking-in occurs after two years of service. Employers must finance at least half of benefits. After retirement, a surviving spouse must receive a pension of at least 60 percent of the member's pension. Before retirement a spouse is entitled to a pension based on the value of the member's vested pension.

CHAPTER 9

Indexing: The Missing Link

EVEN AT A MODEST 4 PERCENT inflation rate, the value of a fixed income is cut in half in eighteen years. At 6 percent, it takes only twelve years. No wonder pensioners worry about the way inflation reduces their incomes.

Fortunately, there is some protection. Government benefits – OAS, Spouse's Allowances, the GIS and CPP/QPP retirement benefits – are adjusted to fully reflect the effects of inflation. And when it comes to the retirement income you provide for yourself, RRIFs in their basic form provide makeshift automatic inflationary increases, as do "escalating" annuities. Unfortunately, when it comes to most employer pensions, you're at the mercy of companies and governments that have more important priorities than inflation- proofing pensions.

Of the eleven pension jurisdictions in Canada, only Ontario is committed to the principle of indexing of pensions, although it certainly doesn't support full indexing.

Pension plans covering members of Parliament, senators, federal civil servants and others under federal jurisdiction are indexed for inflation. Participants make extra contributions for the privilege, although not enough to cover the added cost of the indexed benefit.

A spotty corporate scene

The corporate pension situation, however, is spotty. In 1987, pension benefits consulting firm Hewitt Associates provided a glimpse into the extent of post-retirement inflation indexing of corporate pensions. In a survey of 284 employers in Canada, Hewitt found that 46 percent of employers with defined-benefit pensions (the most common) granted ad hoc increases in 1986 and 70 percent had done so between 1980 and 1984. But increases between 1977 and 1987 had averaged only one-third of increases in the Consumer Price Index.

The year 1987 marked the first time that indexing of pensions became a major issue in labour-management contract negotiations. First, the Canadian Paperworkers Union negotiated a partial-indexing contract with the pulp and paper industry in Eastern Canada. Then the Canadian Auto Workers reached their own deal with the Big Three auto makers. It's likely that unions will keep pushing in this area, but few of them have the clout to make their demands stick.

In Ontario, matters have been helped by the 1987 reform of the province's Pension Benefits Act. The province enshrined the principle of inflation protection for employer pensions and appointed a task force to come up with a formula for applying that principle.

In January 1988, the task force recommended that future pensioners receive annual inflation-proofing to the extent of 75 percent of the increases in the Consumer Price Index, minus one percentage point, with an effective 6.5 percent cap. Citing high costs to employers, the task force stopped short of recommending that those already on pensions should also benefit from the inflation formula. Fourteen months later, the province announced plans for a watered-down version of what the task force had proposed: 75 percent of the Consumer Price Index minus one percentage point on inflation up to 8 percent. But the formula would apply only to 60 percent of "the year's maximum pensionable earnings" ($34,400 in 1993). No further action had been taken by mid-1994.

High hopes for similar legislation in other parts of Canada must be tempered with realism, especially because one of the business arguments against mandatory inflation protection was given added weight by the return of the Mulroney government to power in the November 1988 election.

That election had as its major issue the ratification of the Canada-U.S. free trade agreement, which was assured with the re-election of the Progressive Conservatives. But free trade means stronger competition with U.S. companies hungry for more of the Canadian market, and that does not bode well for pensions. Since Americans are unburdened with inflation-protection legislation, the argument goes, it's not fair to saddle Canadian companies with the added expense.

Laurence Coward, author of the authoritative Mercer Handbook of Canadian Pension and Welfare Plans, says the national pension conference in 1981 reached a consensus that pension reform would have four basic elements: earlier vesting, broader coverage, a better deal for women and inflation protection.

In federal jurisdiction, in Ontario and to some extent elsewhere, three of the four goals have been achieved. To date, however, inflation protection has been the exception. Canadians, and especially unions, will keep pushing for pension indexing. But it isn't realistic to expect mandatory indexing on a national scale in the near future. That's just one more reason why Canadians should think seriously about beefing up their retirement savings.

CHAPTER 10

The Retirement Savings Rules

ALONG WITH THEIR LAST PAY cheque in February 1991, Canadians received their customary T4 slips. This annual tally of the previous year's earnings, tax withheld and other numbers necessary for filing our tax returns. But the 1990 T4 was redesigned and there was a key difference – the addition of box 52 showing the pension adjustment. Because of the potential confusion, Revenue Canada took great care to point out in the tax information package and in newspaper advertisements that the number in box 52 was not for use on 1990 tax returns, as were all the other numbers in the T4 slip. It was to be used by Revenue Canada itself to calculate taxpayers' RRSP "contribution room" for the 1991 taxation year.

The PA is at the heart of a new federal system equating RRSPs and pensions that began a phased introduction in 1991. (The new system should not be confused with the pension reform of the 1980s, a liberalization of provincial and federal pension standards.) The new system sets fairer and more consistent limits on tax assistance, while creating a tax framework to encourage increased private savings for the coming era in the early 2000s when Canada will have a disproportionate number of retired people. At the same time, the new rules are intended to equalize the tax support provided to the three types of vehicles the Income Tax Act endorses to encourage retirement savings.

One type of tax-shelter vehicle is the defined-benefit pension, the most common kind of pension maintained by major companies and governments for their employees. A defined-benefit pension plan projects the amount of pension each employee will receive in retirement, typically based on the employee's earnings and years of service. A second vehicle is the defined-contribution pension, also called money purchase pensions. Under a money purchase plan the employee and employer contributions are deposited in a fund that is used to buy an annuity when the employee retires. You cannot know your pension amount until you retire and purchase your annuity at the prevailing annuity rates. The third vehicle is the RRSP and a less common type of pension called the deferred profit-sharing plan. DPSPs are similar to defined-contribution pensions. (We'll look at the advantages and disadvantages of defined-benefit and defined-contribution pensions in more detail later in this chapter.)

It's helpful to describe the new system by starting with the old. Before 1991, people were never in doubt about the maximum tax-deductible RRSP contributions they were allowed. If they did not belong to a pension or deferred profit-sharing plan they were allowed to contribute and get a deduction for up to 20 percent of earned income to a maximum of $7,500 (using the 1989 and 1990 limits). If they belonged to a pension or profit-sharing plan, they could contribute and deduct up to $3,500 a year (subject to the 20 percent rule) minus their pension contribution. The smaller contribution limit took into account an assumed employer contribution.

Though it made it easy for people to figure out the RRSP contributions they were allowed each year, the old system was flawed. People with defined-benefit pensions received more in tax support (largely through deductions to employers and employees) than people who had only RRSPs and/or defined-contribution pensions. That was unfair and discriminatory. The new system will attempt to equalize the tax support provided to each type of retirement vehicle by 1995.

This is being done in two ways. The potential RRSP contribution limit is being increased and the actual contribution has been restricted to no more than 18 percent of earned income. A narrower definition of earned income starting in 1991 is part of the changes as well. The definition of "earned income" is broader than income which you earn. Your earned income has to be adjusted for rental income and for the receipt or payment of alimony. In 1994 the maximum RRSP contribution is $13,500 and is scheduled to rise by $1,000 a year until it reaches $15,500. After 1996, increases in the RRSP contribution limit will be indexed to average wage increases. Prior to the February 1994 federal budget, there were rumours that the RRSP limits would be lowered. However, the government simply announced its intention to review the retirement income system in Canada. Watch for changes in the future.

The other mechanism for equalizing tax support for people in pensions and those with RRSPs is through the PA. In working out your RRSP contribution room each year, Revenue Canada will start with the lesser of the year's maximum deductible RRSP contribution and 18 per cent of the previous year's earned income. It will then deduct the previous year's PA. The resultant figure, subject to adjustments in some cases, will be your RRSP contribution room.

Why has the government changed the maximum RRSP contribution from 20 percent to 18 percent of earned income? In fact, that's a change the government and its consultants spent a good deal of time addressing. It was observed that the average career length is thirty-five years and a decent retirement income is 70 percent of an employee's final pay, with continuing benefits for the surviving spouse and reasonable inflation protection. After examining wage patterns and investment returns during this century, the government decided that a person needs to save about 18 percent of earnings each year to achieve this level of retirement income. To avoid providing too much tax support to the well-to-do, it was further decided that 18 percent of annual income was a reasonable figure up to 2.5 times the average industrial wage.

The new rule book is complex, but employers and Revenue Canada do most of the extra work. No longer do you have to calculate your allowable RRSP contributions. Like a user-friendly interface used in personal computers to mask the complexity that is actually necessary in electronic calculations, the revised pension system is user-friendly to Jane and John Canuck while leaving the complications to employers and Revenue Canada.

The PA is the value used by Revenue Canada to measure your pension benefits for the year. It gives Revenue Canada a basis for working out your annual RRSP contribution room, a figure that the department will provide to you in your annual notice of assessment regarding your income tax return. (To individuals it has little meaning except that the lower it is, the more RRSP contribution room you have. As we'll see in a moment, you can figure out the PA yourself so you can contribute to your RRSP early in the year and not risk exceeding your limit.)

There was a second serious problem with the old system: if you did not make your allowable RRSP contributions each year you lost the right to make that eligible contribution forever. Even if during your peak earning years you could afford to make up for missed contributions of past years, the law did not permit it. This has changed. Starting in 1991, you may carry forward unused RRSP contributions for up to seven years, or more in some cases.

You will receive a notice of assessment after Revenue Canada has reviewed your income tax return. This assessment will tell you how much you can contribute to your RRSP and claim on your next tax return. You have plenty of time to make your contributions; in fact you have until March 1 of the next year. However, it is advisable to contribute early rather than late in the year so that your money starts earning tax-sheltered interest as soon as possible. Consistently making your RRSP contributions early in the year can increase your RRSP nest egg by thousands of dollars.

You don't have to wait until you receive your notice of contribution room from Revenue Canada; you can still contribute early. You can begin contributing to your RRSP the first week of the New Year. After receiving your T4 slip in late February, you can work out your own RRSP contribution room for that year and adjust your contributions for the rest of the year if your RRSP contribution room doesn't match the pattern of savings you've already established. You could then look at your notice of assessment from Revenue Canada to confirm that the contribution you have already made during the year was at least in the ball park.

Let's walk through an example for 1994. Suppose you had 1993 earned income of $40,000 and your PA was $3,000. (Remember, you use the earned income of the previous year.) Start your calculation by multiplying the $40,000 by 18 percent. You have $7,200. Now deduct the $3,000 PA. Your RRSP contribution room for 1994 is $4,200. If your contribution room is more than the year's potential contribution limit ($13,500 in 1994), you must stick to the lower amount. For example, if your PA was $500 and earned income $80,000, you would multiply the $80,000 by 18 percent, deduct the PA and find that the contribution room of $13,900 exceeds the RRSP contribution limit. If this was the case, you deduct the PA from the $13,500 and your contribution room would be $13,000.

Because you could make a mistake in the calculation, the amended rules allow each RRSP holder a penalty-free lifetime over-contribution of $8,000. Instead of hitting us with an interest penalty on each dollar contributed over the annual limit, the $8,000 over-contribution limit provides room for error.

This can be a rewarding error to make. The extra money contributed compounds over the years, along with the rest of your RRSP funds. And while an excess contribution is not deductible that year, you may be able to deduct it in future as new RRSP room is created.

Ian Markham, a partner in Peat Marwick Thorne Actuarial and Benefits Inc. in Toronto, feels the new system, despite its complexity and few remaining inequities, is much fairer than the old. "While it's not perfect," Markham says, "the rewritten rules provide all taxpayers with the opportunity to build up a sizable tax-assisted pension, regardless of whether they are fortunate enough to work for an employer that has a generous pension plan. The system also shows you, via the annual Revenue Canada statement, roughly how much you should be contributing to your RRSP each year in order to retire on a pension of around 70 percent of your final pay (including any employer pension). The Canadian population is aging, and we cannot rely totally on the government to pay our pension, because our children will not be willing to bear the resulting tax burden."

Since the new rules make the administration of defined-benefit plans more complex than in the past, the simplicity of money purchase plans may look even more appealing to employers. The increase in contribution limits for money purchase pensions also helps make them more palatable.

As a result, some defined-benefit pension plans are being converted to the money purchase variety, and few new defined-benefit plans are being set up. That's unfortunate, because the strength of defined-benefit pensions from the employee's viewpoint is that, when interest rates are low, the risk of retiring is shifted to the employer's shoulders. With money purchase plans, lower interest rates at retirement time hurt employees who are faced with annuities that pay less. Conversely, retirees gain if rates are high.

The money purchase concept, as already mentioned, also underlies a lesser-known retirement savings vehicle, the deferred profit-sharing plan (DPSP). With a DPSP, employer contributions are related to profits. The minimum requirement is that the employer contribute at least 1 percent of the remuneration of participating employees in any year when the firm makes a profit. As with other money purchase pensions, the DPSP either buys a life annuity for the retiring employee or is transferred to an RRSP for purchasing a

RRIF. DPSP contributions by an employer also reduce employees' allowable RRSP contributions.

A changing picture

A survey of employer pension plans conducted by benefits consulting firm Actrex Partners Ltd. provides some insight into how pension reform has changed the Canadian pension picture as of July 1, 1988.

The Actrex survey of ninety-one employers, ranging from those with fewer than 100 pension plan members to those with more than 10,000, found that 9 percent of plan members belonged to money purchase pensions. But the startling finding was that 52 percent of plans affecting 73 percent of employees were fully employer-funded. This result contrasted with an Actrex survey two years earlier that found only 36 percent of plans covering 17 percent of employees were non-contributory.

The trend toward money purchase pensions is not just due to the fact that increasing contribution limits reduce the tax bias in favour of defined-benefit plans. Money purchase plans also neatly sidestep two expensive problems for employers in defined-benefit plans.

One problem is the current legal wrangling over whether any surplus belongs to the employer or the employees. With money purchase pensions, there usually is no surplus. The other problem is the mandating of partial inflation indexing that Ontario plans to pioneer. With a money purchase pension, retired employees simply get less initially to pay for increases later.

As for the jump in the number of non-contributory defined-benefit plans, this development appears to solve problems for employers without creating any for employees. While administrative complexity doesn't disappear, things are somewhat simpler for employers because there is no need to keep detailed records of employee contributions.

In a sense, whether a pension plan is contributory or not is a matter of semantics. The money all comes out of the same pot. To the employer, it makes little difference whether employees are paid more so they can contribute to the pension, or paid less, with the company contributing the difference in addition to its own share.

CHAPTER 11

Questions to Ask Your Employer

IF YOU BELONG TO A PENSION plan, how much do you know about it? Chances are, not much.

Many people have a sound grasp of RRSPs, mortgages and banking services, but only the sketchiest knowledge of their employer pensions. Yet for a person who has worked many years for one employer, a pension is often worth more than RRSPs and government benefits combined. That's why it's wise to start asking questions and to pay attention to your periodic statement of pension benefits. Make sure you understand how your pension will dovetail with other income.

Some employers hold extensive information sessions for people approaching retirement, even calling in outside experts. Others take a more casual approach. Even if your employer is willing to help, don't assume that all your needs and wants will automatically be met. Here are some typical questions, along with background information, that you might care to put to your employer.

Q: In retiring at the usual age of sixty-five, what's the normal option? What are some others?
A: If you're married, federal or provincial law will often dictate a joint-and-last-survivor pension of at least 60 percent of the full amount to protect your surviving spouse (see Chapter Eight), unless you opt out of this standard treatment by jointly signing a waiver. Otherwise, the usual options are:
- A pension for your life.
- A pension for life but with a five-, ten- or fifteen-year guarantee for the benefit of your spouse, estate or children.
- A joint-and-last-survivor pension that would continue to be paid to your spouse if you should die first.

The first option provides the highest pension, while the third provides the lowest benefits. You should choose the joint-and-last-survivor option if your spouse would otherwise have inadequate income. The first two may be preferable if you have a large insurance policy with your spouse as beneficiary, or if your spouse has independent income. The greater the age difference between you and your younger spouse, the greater the reduction in payouts under the joint-and-last-survivor option. Note that joint-and-last-survivor options apply only to your spouse at the time of retirement. Should your spouse die before you, and you remarry after retirement, your second spouse is not entitled to the benefit.

Q: Can I make the decision on survivor options at any time?
A: Generally, you can decide at any time close to retirement, say within a year. In some cases you can decide earlier. But once retired, you're locked in.

Q: What about survivor rights of common-law spouses?
A: In 1988, the federal government redefined "spouse" to include a common-law partner of the opposite sex with whom you have lived for at least one year. The change means that a qualifying common-law spouse is entitled to the same survivor benefits as a spouse through marriage, whether the benefits are from a pension plan, DPSP, an annuity purchased with RRSP funds or a RRIF. If you die before your common-law spouse, he or she is also entitled to a tax-free transfer of your RRSP funds to his or her own RRSP.

Q. Is a life income fund (LIF) available to me as a retirement option?
A. Possibly, depending upon your province of residence and whether your pension plan allows for it. Take a look at chapter 28 for more information on LIFs.

Q: How do children become pension beneficiaries?
A: If you and your spouse both die and there's a guarantee, your children can get the remaining pension payments. Consult your employer for options under your plan.

Q: I've heard of "integrated" pension benefits. What are they?
A: In the periodic statements issued by defined-benefit pension plans, the CPP/QPP retirement benefit is almost always integrated into the total figure. OAS is not integrated.

Q: I'm told we have a "final-average" pension plan where I work. What does that mean?
A: It means you're fortunate. A final-average plan is a particular type of defined-benefit pension (the term doesn't apply to money

purchase pensions) in which your initial annual pension income is calculated on the basis of a percentage (often 2 percent) multiplied by the years of service and by the average earnings for the last five years (or sometimes the five years when you earned the most). This is usually subject to integration with CPP/QPP benefits. If you have thirty years of service with your employer and averaged $35,000 a year in the last five (or your best five) years, your pension plus CPP retirement benefits under a 2 percent formula would total .02 x 30 x $35,000, or $21,000.

Traditional career-average pension plans average your career earnings, so the pension will usually be less than with a final-average formula. However, modern career-average pensions typically will increase benefits periodically to reflect recent earnings, and your pension may not be much less than under a final-average formula. It could even be more.

Q: It's quite a drop to $21,000 from $35,000? Should I consider that a good pension?
A: It's not bad, once the figure is put into perspective. For one thing, this amount doesn't include OAS. For another, people often can get by in retirement on less income. That's because many expenses are lower. For instance, the costs of work clothing and travel to work are eliminated. Also, the Income Tax Act offers tax breaks to pensioners through the age credit and the pension income credit.

Q: But how can you equate pre-retirement income and expenses with post-retirement income and expenses?
A: The answer is the "net income replacement calculation," which many large employers will work out for you. This calculation tells you in after-tax terms what proportion of your final year's earnings you'll be pulling in after retirement. Typically, you might find that your gross income in the first year after retirement is only 62 percent of your gross income in the year before retirement, but this works out to a more manageable 76 percent after tax.

Q: I make higher contributions to my pension than the plan requires. How will I be credited with the extra money when I retire?
A: In the past, many pension plans permitted additional voluntary contributions (AVCs) for past or current service. They were tax-deductible, within limits. Past-service contributions haven't been allowed since 1986, but AVCs for current service are still permissible if your pension plan allows them, and they remain deductible.

AVCs reduce what you may contribute to an RRSP. The nice thing about AVCs is their flexibility at retirement. You don't have to lump them with your basic pension created from mandatory contributions. At retirement or at any time before your seventy-first birthday, you may instead take the AVCs and the interest they generate in cash (a poor choice, since you'd pay tax on the whole amount) or transfer the money directly to an RRSP. When you collapse the RRSP consisting of AVC money, you can purchase a RRIF or an annuity. With a RRIF, you can continue to make investment decisions – a right you don't usually have with pension.

Q: What about inflation indexing?
A: OAS and CPP retirement benefits are fully indexed to offset inflation. And although Ontario plans to require partial indexing, there is no legislation anywhere in Canada to compel employers to index pensions. However, some employers provide occasional ad hoc increases to help protect retired employees against inflation.

You could ask whether your pension plan is "in surplus" – that is, does it have more than the minimum needed to cover its obligations. Although there is no guarantee, a plan with a surplus is more likely to spring for increases, especially if it has done so in the past.

Q: I belong to a company pension plan and would like to retire early. What's involved?
A: Under federal and Ontario pension standards laws, you are allowed to retire up to ten years before the usual age of sixty-five and receive benefits from vested pensions. Of course, an early pension is reduced in recognition of the lesser contributions and the longer period it will be paid out.

In other jurisdictions, make inquiries. Some employers have stated policies; others have trimmed staffs in recent years by offering incentives for employees to retire early. A common early-retirement option, sometimes called the level-income option, integrates your employer pension with government benefits. You might be able to retire at age sixty with a company pension that will be reduced by OAS and CPP retirement benefits when they kick in.

OAS benefits begin at age sixty-five. But you can choose to take CPP retirement benefits as early as age sixty if you "substantially" leave the work force, or as late as age seventy if you keep working. You would receive up to 30 percent less if retiring early but up to 30 percent more if you keep working until seventy.

Q: I'd like to work until age seventy or so. How about late retirement?

A: That's up to your employer. Some employers would be delighted to have you stay on; others would prefer that you to retire on schedule. See the above item about taking CPP retirement benefits late if you keep working. And remember, there's nothing preventing you from taking the CPP benefit at sixty-five while remaining on the job.

Q: What will my spouse receive if I die before my scheduled retirement?

A: Your surviving spouse will at least get a lump-sum return of your contributions, along with interest (unless the plan is non-contributory). Depending on age, he or she would be well advised to transfer the money to an RRSP or buy an annuity or RRIF. Generous pensions will provide your spouse with your full pension starting at the time you would have turned sixty-five. Ask your employer about the provisions of your plan and refer to Chapter Eight for information on federal and provincial law governing survivor benefits.

Q: How about electronic depositing of cheques?

A: Increasingly, employers and insurance companies making annuity and RRIF payments are offering this service. It's something you'll appreciate during a postal strike or snowstorm.

Q: What about having income tax deducted at source?

A: You're probably used to having tax taken out before you see your pay cheque, but during retirement things are different. Although tax is withheld on employer pension payments of at least $500 a month, that's not so with income from annuities, RRIFs (except when you take out more than the minimum RRIF payments set by law), OAS or CPP payments. You are required to make quarterly tax installments to Revenue Canada if at least 75 percent of your income is not subject to withholding at source and you owe at least $2,000 in tax for the year.

This will please many people because it means they can collect interest on their money until it's time to pay an installment. Others would rather have tax taken out of their pension cheques. You can have this done, in $5 units, by filling in Revenue Canada's personal tax credit return, Form TD1. Your company's payroll department has it on hand; just complete the form and hand it back.

The TD1 is used to determine the amount of tax your employer deducts from your pay. Question 18 on the form asks whether you want tax deductions increased from the amount you must to pay.

Q: Do you have group life insurance at work?
A: If so, ask about having it converted to a pay-yourself basis after retirement. Before you make the switch check the cost of competing policies. Converting a group policy is often prohibitively expensive.

Q: Have you any tax tips?
A: We certainly do. You have the right to split CPP income equally with your spouse. You must be at least sixty years of age to receive CPP retirement benefits, and your spouse has to be at least sixty before you can share this income. There's no advantage to splitting the credits if you and your spouse are in the same tax bracket. But if you're in different brackets, it's worth while splitting the credits to get more income into the hands of the spouse who will pay less tax.

Apply at your local Income Security Programs office of Health and Welfare Canada (under "H" in the blue Government of Canada pages at the back of your local telephone directory).

Another excellent strategy also uses the "income splitting" principle, although this one will only be possible for one more year. If you're receiving income from an employer pension or DPSP and your spouse has not turned seventy-one, you can transfer up to $6,000 to a spousal RRSP. Unfortunately, 1994 is the last year for this. Remember, this is in addition to your usual annual contribution limits.

Finally, many civil servants and corporate executives receive retiring allowances. Unused sick days are also sometimes converted to cash at retirement. There would be a hefty tax bite if you had to take a large retirement allowance into income at one time, so the Income Tax Act allows you to defer tax by rolling set amounts into your RRSP beyond your usual annual contribution limits.

For 1989 and subsequent years, there's a limit of $2,000 for each calendar year of service. For service before 1989, it's $2,000 for each calendar year, plus $1,500 more for each calendar year when you did not belong to the employer's pension plan or DPSP. A "calendar year" for rollovers can be much less than twelve months. For instance, if you started employment in November or December of a particular year, that year counts as if it were a full twelve months.

If you'll be receiving a retiring allowance, it's a good idea to have your employer transfer the money directly to your RRSP. Otherwise, tax will be withheld until you file your next tax return. Despite the tax-free roll-over of the retiring allowance, Revenue Canada may still get a crack at you. The money rolled into RRSPs from retiring allowances counts as income in calculating the alternative minimum tax, a provision designed to keep the well-to-do from sheltering too much of their income from tax. The task of easing the tax blow in your retirement year is discussed in chapter 34.

CHAPTER 12

What Do Pensions Leave for Your Estate?

IF YOU ARE LIKE MOST prospective retirees, you're probably wondering what happens to your pension when you die.

Whether you're married or widowed, single or divorced, there's a good chance that nothing will be left to your family unless you get counselling from your employer or an outside advisor before you decide on your pension options.

Your first major decision is whether leaving an estate is important to you. If it is, you can elect pension payments with a guarantee period of up to fifteen years or the years remaining until your eighty-sixth birthday, whichever is less. Ten- or fifteen-year guarantees are commonly chosen.

Payments can continue

The significance of the guarantee is that if you die before the end of the period – or, if you're married, have chosen the usual joint-life option and both you and your spouse die before the guarantee is up – payments can continue to a beneficiary.

A common situation would be choosing a joint-and-last-survivor pension with a fifteen-year guarantee under the options your employer pension provides. If you and your spouse have both died by the tenth year, and you've named your daughter as beneficiary, she would receive your pension cheques for five years.

This is something that can't be done with either a RRIF or an annuity bought with RRSP funds. If you use RRSP proceeds to buy a RRIF or a joint-life annuity with a guarantee, the money left will normally be taxed as a lump sum in your estate.

The right to leave pension money to a beneficiary under a guarantee does not come without a cost. You must accept lower pension payments for this privilege, just as you must for a joint-and-last-survivor option. But the difference in income is often relatively small. If you're interested, ask your employer for monthly income figures under different guarantee periods. The beneficiary doesn't have to be a relative or even a person. It can be your church, synagogue or a charity.

CHAPTER 13

Winding Down Your RRSP

RRIFS, LIFs AND ANNUITIES are hot topics among people in their sixties and seventies. Whether at the golf course or seniors' centre, any discussion of winding down an RRSP creates plenty of interest. And so it should. Investing in RRIFs, LIFs and annuities is likely the biggest financial decision you will make during your retirement.

For most of the rest of the book we'll walk you through the world of RRIFs, LIFs and annuities. You'll learn about your options and read valuable tips to help you avoid costly mistakes. But first, let's talk a little about the years leading up to your RRIF and annuity decisions – a time when making the right decisions with your RRSPs can be more crucial than ever.

RRSPs are the most important and most widely used tax shelter available to Canadians. Through RRSPs, we can put away retirement savings for many years while the money grows. The tax deductions we get for contributions are not only an incentive to contribute, but a bonus that allows us to contribute more than we could otherwise afford.

The whole point of RRSPs is to save for retirement. And what do we do with the accumulated money? Spend it, of course. Just as we live on our salaries while we're still working, we live on our government pensions, employer pensions and RRSP savings when we retire. We're not talking about blowing the money; we're talking about spending it in an orderly fashion – and with the same discipline that is necessary to save it in the first place. We must make sure it lasts the rest of our lives. That's the central theme of this book.

Be flexible
But before we can spend the money, it must be converted into a retirement income option – a RRIF, an annuity or some combination

that will provide us with regular payments. This is something the law says we must do by the end of the year when we reach seventy-one, so the timing of the move from RRSPs to annuities and/or RRIFs or LIFs is important.

In the years approaching retirement, when you know you will be setting up a RRIF, LIF or an annuity – and especially around age seventy-one – be flexible with your RRSPs. You'll want your money to be available when you decide to arrange your income.

Let's take the example of a non-redeemable term deposit or guaranteed investment certificate (GIC) available at many financial institutions. You may have chosen a five-year investment term and decided after three years, when interest rates happen to be high, that you want to buy an annuity. Unfortunately, this type of RRSP does not usually allow you to redeem your GIC before maturity, although some institutions will let you have the cash in return for an interest-rate penalty.

Let's say you're earning 8 percent on your five-year certificate and interest rates shoot up to 10 percent. You need more pension income, and your RRSP is an obvious source. But you can't get the money out, so you can't take advantage of high annuity rates. Alternatively, you may be able to get your money, but subject to an adjustment that results in a lesser amount for your annuity or RRIF.

It is far better to deal with a financial institution that will let you break the term of your RRSP, or to have an RRSP that is flexible in itself. For example, you might have a self-administered RRSP of which some portion is in readily cashable Canada Savings Bonds or treasury bills.

It's not always necessary to stay in low-interest investments to have this flexibility. You could, for example, invest in mutual funds or in a self-administered plan holding stocks that could be changed to a RRIF at any time.

However, for the majority of people who invest in term-deposit-style RRSPs – that is, those offering specific guaranteed interest rates for periods of one to five years – there are plans that will allow early redemptions or simply a conversion to an annuity, RRIF or LIF. This remains a valuable option when interest rates are unstable and you don't know when you'll need income from your RRSPs.

If you don't need to get at your RRSP and don't see any potential need to do so, the selection of financial institutions handling RRSP contributions is wide open. But if you're in your sixties, be sure you understand what flexibility you have.

RRIFs, LIFs and annuities as pensions

Then you can get down to the serious business of RRIFs, LIFs and annuities. When you do, it's best to start thinking of these retirement income vehicles as pensions. While an actuary will tell you there are subtle distinctions, an annuity, RRIF or LIF simply pays you periodic income in retirement – which is just what a pension does.

At one time, you had to be least sixty to start receiving annuity or RRIF income, but that restriction has been removed. If you choose to retire in your fifties, you can use your RRSP as a source of RRIF or annuity income.

Even so, there are many people who think they must wait until age seventy-one to make a decision on what to do with their RRSP funds. From a tax viewpoint, it may indeed be the best strategy, but there's a financial adage that says you shouldn't let the tax tail wag the financial dog. Review your cash and RRSP investments at this point. Then decide which source of income will be the most tax-effective.

Obviously, if you need income when you retire, look to your RRSPs. What's wrong with enjoying the income while you're younger and perhaps better able to do so? The years from fifty-five to seventy-five will be your most active in terms of leisure activity, and extra income could come in quite handy. After seventy-five, such activity tends to taper off, and so do expenses.

Enjoy the ride

Sure, you should plan for the future – that's what this book is about. But you should also enjoy the ride, and sometimes the extra income from a RRIF or annuity is all it takes to make the trip more pleasurable.

The most important consideration by far in buying an annuity, LIF or RRIF is choosing the investment or combination of investments that suits you – you can buy as many annuities and RRIFs and LIFs as you wish. A wrong decision could affect your income while you are living, as well as that of your surviving spouse if you die. In addition, there could be little or nothing left for your family or estate.

There are five directions you can take when you wind down your RRSPs. You can:

- Cash the RRSPs in a lump sum or over a period of years;
- Buy a single-life annuity on your life alone;
- Buy a joint-and-last-survivor annuity;
- Buy a fixed-term (also called a term-certain) annuity to age ninety;
- Buy a RRIF.

Locked-in RRSPs can be converted to annuities or LIFs – more on this in a later chapter. Keep in mind as we examine each option in the rest of *Retire Right* that you can choose any combination of options as part of a strategy to meet your retirement needs.

Cashing your RRSP

When you arrange an annuity or a RRIF, your RRSP is transferred to the plan without incurring any immediate income tax burden. Keep in mind that you will have to pay tax on funds as they are withdrawn.

The idea of paying any tax at all on your savings may seem odd. But remember, it has not been taxed previously. You received tax deductions for your contributions and your money grew unhindered by taxes. Therefore, you owe tax when it comes out, whether the withdrawals are in lump sums or in monthly payments from an annuity or RRIF.

Taking cash out of your RRSP without going the RRIF or annuity route is seldom wise unless you're in a very low tax bracket. Whether you take out a lump sum or spread smaller withdrawals over several years, the money is added to your income for the year and you will pay tax. You could even be propelled into a higher tax bracket.

Let's take the example of Frank, a single pensioner in Ontario. In 1988 he had $20,000 in income from pensions and Canada Savings Bond interest. After personal tax credits, Frank would have paid $2,556 in tax.

We said "would have." Frank cashed in a $15,000 RRSP, bumping his income to $35,000. Frank's tax bill for 1988 was $7,523 – almost $5,000 more than he would have paid without the RRSP withdrawal.

Why the big increase? Frank's RRSP withdrawal not only results in more tax; taking the lump sum into income pushes him into a higher tax bracket. He pays one-third of the RRSP funds to Revenue Canada.

The income tax owed when an RRSP is collapsed is often confused with the tax withheld by the financial institution when the RRSP is cashed. This mandatory withholding, which may be more or less than you owe on the money withdrawn, is simply an interim payment.

No one knows how much tax you owe until you file a tax return. You can refer to Table VII for amounts that will be withheld when you cash in your RRSP.

Be careful you don't do what Frank's friend Bob did the year before. He assumed that because he was taking only $5,000 out of his RRSP and there was only a 10 percent withholding at this level that he wouldn't owe more tax when he filed his return.

It was an unpleasant surprise to learn that he did owe more money at the end of April.

Despite the general caveat that it's not a good idea to take chunks out of your RRSP, cashing the plan in stages before the end of your seventy-first year can be effective for some people. If you confine your withdrawals to the amount an annuity or RRIF would provide, you would be in the same position from a tax viewpoint. You might consider this approach if you feel you're not ready to tie yourself down to a structured RRIF or annuity. Once you reach seventy-one, however, you'll have to make a decision.

Withholding Taxes

The trustee of your RRSP must withhold tax from any amount withdrawn by you in cash. The tax withheld may be claimed as a credit on your income tax return as taxes paid in the year. The withholding tax rate is based on the amount withdrawn:

	All provinces except Quebec	P.Q. only
$5,000 or less	10%	18%
$5,001 – $15,000	20%	30%
$15,001 or more	30%	35%

You can minimize the tax withheld at source by keeping any cash withdrawals to $5,000 or less. Note that withholding tax is simply a prepayment of tax and an additional tax liability may result, depending upon your tax bracket when you file your return.

TABLE VII

Some people systematically withdraw cash from their RRSPs until age seventy-one, then continue doing the same thing through a RRIF. For example, at age sixty-five you could plan to take out all your money over ten years by using RRSP withdrawals until age seventy-one and RRIF withdrawals after that. While this strategy wouldn't suit most people, it can meet the needs of some.

Before undertaking any sort of cash withdrawals, think long term. Cashing your RRSP may bring only short-term happiness. Many people tend to fritter away lump sums without considering that they may still be around twenty or thirty years from now – and in need of money.

CHAPTER 14

Just What Is an Annuity?

IMAGINE YOU'RE IN THE market for a house. You find just what you're looking for, and at $100,000 the price is a bargain. You have a 50 percent down payment and are prepared to take on a mortgage for $50,000.

You decide on a twenty-five year amortization period and lock in the interest rate at 8.75 percent for the entire term. (For the sake of this illustration, let's ignore the reality of mortgage renewals.) Your bank manager tells you the blended monthly payments – consisting of principal and interest – will be $405.81. As you leave the manager's office, his parting words are: "Don't worry. Just 300 payments and you'll have no mortgage."

Years later, you're sixty-five and in the market for an annuity. You have $50,000 in your RRSP. After reviewing your requirements with a RRIF/annuity broker, you settle on a fixed-term (also known as term-certain) annuity to age ninety. The annuity will provide you with a monthly income for twenty-five years, for a total of 300 payments. The broker cautions that your annuity will run out in your ninetieth year. At 8.75 percent interest, your monthly income will be $405.81. As you leave her office, she says: "Good luck in your retirement. You have a twenty-five year pension to enjoy."

A mortgage in reverse

That's right: an annuity is a mortgage in reverse. In the case of a mortgage, a financial institution provides you with a lump sum that you repay over a period of years, with interest. In the case of an annuity, you provide the company with the lump sum and it pays you back over a period of years, also with interest.

Interest-rate assumptions underlying annuities are based on long-term rates because the company invests your money for a long term, often in bonds. In later chapters of *Retire Right* you'll also see how life expectancy is tied to annuity rates in single-life and joint-life annuities.

Before we get into the nitty-gritty of annuities, however, here's a thought: while RRIFs provide the marvelous flexibility that has made them justly popular – a subject we'll explore in detail in the next section of the book – annuities are better for some people in some situations.

The only way to decide what's right for you is to compare retirement options and their features. As intimidating as they might appear, computer printouts can show you how much income you would have at various ages if you go with one product or the other.

Not all financial institutions will give you this side-by-side comparison for the simple reason that not all are allowed by law to offer all products. Only life insurance companies can sell life annuities, although they also offer term-certain annuities, LIFs and RRIFs. Trust companies and banks can offer term-certain annuities, LIFs and RRIFs, while stockbrokers, mutual fund dealers and credit unions can market only LIFs and RRIFs. If you hear unfavourable comments about annuities, consider who is making the comments.

CHAPTER 15

Your Annuity Choices

IN THIS CHAPTER, WE WILL take a look at some of the choices you face when considering annuities, and some of the factors that will influence your decision. First, let's examine the term-certain annuity to age ninety in greater detail.

You saw in the last chapter that for a sixty-five-year-old, a term-certain annuity to age ninety is the reverse of a twenty-five-year mortgage. Under this option, also known as a fixed-term annuity to age ninety, income continues to your ninetieth year. If you die before then, your surviving spouse will continue receiving payments until the year in which you would have turned ninety. Or if your spouse is younger, you can choose an age-to-ninety annuity based on your spouse's birth date.

Take the case of Tom, seventy-one, and his sixty-five-year-old wife, Betty. Tom is winding down his RRSP and he can choose either a nineteen-year or twenty-five-year stream of payments. The income from the latter is smaller, but provides six more years of protection for Betty.

Table VIII shows the monthly income available in July 1994 from a $50,000 RRSP for men and women aged sixty through seventy-one. Since Tom is seventy-one, the nineteen-year annuity would pay him $442.33 monthly. If he elects Betty's age ninety, the twenty-five-year annuity would pay $402.52 monthly.

If you are convinced you won't live beyond ninety, the term-certain annuity may be for you. But it doesn't offer protection should you live to a ripe old age.

Roughly one in six people who are sixty-five today will live to ninety. Do you really want to take a chance on living to that age, only to find yourself in financial difficulty? Consider your total financial picture and health before deciding on any alternative.

Typical Income from Various Annuities

The following table illustrates the monthly income from annuities that a $50,000 RRSP will provide at certain ages.

Age at Purchase	Single-Life 10-Year Guarantee Male	Single-Life 10-Year Guarantee Female	Joint-Life 10-Year Guarantee Male & Female	Term-Certain To Age 90 Male & Female
60	424.47	402.90	382.24	382.93
61	429.85	407.35	385.74	386.53
62	434.98	411.76	388.97	389.44
63	440.72	416.70	393.28	393.34
64	446.90	422.00	397.08	397.19
65	453.26	427.21	401.76	402.52
66	459.94	433.45	406.29	407.34
67	466.86	439.61	411.59	413.49
68	473.98	446.21	417.63	419.68
69	481.28	453.04	423.39	426.46
70	488.71	460.37	429.95	434.11
71	496.25	467.76	436.79	442.33

All monthly incomes start one month after purchase date.

SOURCE: CANNEX, JULY 1994

TABLE VIII

If you are definitely not concerned about living beyond ninety, the term-certain annuity to age ninety offers an important advantage: it provides a greater estate value than other types of annuities for a person who dies at average life expectancy. Alternatively, if you were to decide to cash the annuity, you could easily determine the commuted value of the annuity to ninety at any time.

For example, let's assume that at age seventy-one you buy a term-certain annuity to age ninety with $50,000 of RRSP money. At your approximate life expectancy of eighty-two, you then decide to cash the annuity. While we'll go into more detail later on how the company arrives at the cash figure, the value might be about $30,952 at 1994 interest rates.

For those worried about the age dilemma, a life annuity with a minimum guarantee period to age ninety, which is discussed in the next section, may be a better solution. It would pay beyond age ninety if you're still living and you don't sacrifice much for this feature.

The term-certain annuity to age ninety is available from life insurance companies and a few trust companies and banks. It is the only type of annuity that offers payments for a specific number of years without any lifetime or joint-life continuation beyond that period.

The term-certain annuity is a reasonable alternative to the joint-and-last-survivor type. You can see from Table VIII how the payments under this plan compare with the various survivor options. The monthly income from the joint-and-last-survivor annuity is only a few dollars more a month than that from the term-certain annuity to ninety.

Table IX is a survey of the monthly term-certain annuity income offered by life insurance companies and banks in return for $50,000 of RRSP funds owned by a sixty-five-year-old man or woman. These numbers vary from week to week, and one company may be more competitive than another at a given time.

Term-Certain-to-Age-Ninety Annuity Market Survey

MALE OR FEMALE, AGE 65
$50,000 RRSP

Company	Monthly Income
Mutual Life of Canada	$404.05
Transamerica Life	404.02
Allstate Life	403.84
Sun Life of Canada	401.21
Bank of Nova Scotia	399.84
Standard Life	399.37
Canada Life	395.75
Metropolitan Life	394.27
Industrial Alliance	393.44
North West Life	393.44
Laurier Life Ins. Co.	393.09
North American Life.	393.05
Confederation Life	392.91
Manulife Financial	390.85
Imperial Life	390.53
NN Financial	388.09
Crown Life	386.76
Great West Life	380.08
Empire Life	358.28
Royal Life	328.64

SOURCE: CANNEX, JULY 1994

TABLE IX

You should note that although deposits at banks and trust companies are covered by the federal government's Canada Deposit Insurance Corporation, this insurance does not extend to term-certain annuities offered by these institutions. Neither are any life insurance company annuities covered by CDIC insurance, although life insurers must adhere to strict solvency requirements and now insure annuities up to $2,000 per month with any one institution. (Chapter 30 looks at How Safe Is Your Money?)

Life annuities

Over time, the life annuity has been much maligned and often misunderstood. Yet for many years the single-life version was the most common option chosen by people retiring with employer pension plans. Why the seeming contradiction? Largely because many retirees of ten to fifteen years ago were given no other alternative than the single-life annuity. Now that other options are available, those retiring today have more financial choices. But the life annuity still merits serious consideration.

Income from a life annuity lasts your lifetime. If you live to 105, a life annuity continues to pay – despite a common misconception that all annuities stop paying at age ninety. In its riskiest form, a life annuity stops paying the day you die. Known as a straight-life annuity, life-only annuity or life annuity with no guarantee, it's the kind Uncle Harry chose from his company pension plan and, when he died three months later, left no income for Aunt Eleanor. Everyone was up in arms at the time, and rightly so.

Fortunately, few people choose this type of life annuity these days. In fact, most life insurance companies – the only financial institutions able to offer the life annuity – require that a person who insists on a straight-life annuity indicate he is aware of the risks he is taking by signing a form indicating that he or she is aware payments stop at death.

In addition to the security of a lifetime income, most life annuities include a guaranteed minimum number of payments. If you die before receiving these payments, they go to your surviving spouse. This includes a common-law spouse with whom you have lived for at least a year.

You will see from Table VIII that monthly incomes from annuities differ for men and women of the same age. Because women live longer than men on average, the insurance company expects to pay women longer. So it pays them less each month.

Some people see this practice as discriminatory. In the case of employer pension plans, some Canadian jurisdictions agree. In Ontario and under federal regulations, a woman gets the same pension as a man with the same work experience. This applies only to pension accruals since 1987.

Which pays more?

A commonly asked question is whether a single annuity for a certain amount pays more than two annuities for the same amount – for example, one $50,000 annuity as opposed to two $25,000 annuities. The answer is yes. This is because a life insurance company has fixed costs for issuing a contract, and whether the contract is for $50,000 or $25,000, the expense is the same.

Comparing Annuities of Various Amounts

MALE, AGE 65 LIFE ONLY

Amount of RRSP	Monthly Income
$10,000	$ 93.86
25,000	238.72
50,000	481.32
100,000	969.29
250,000	2,460.54

SOURCE: CANNEX, JULY 1994

TABLE X

In our example, two annuities worth $25,000 each on a life-only basis for a man of sixty-five will pay a total of about $477.44 monthly. A $50,000 annuity would pay about $481.32, or $3.88 more. At higher amounts, such as $100,000 and over, the monthly income increases to a greater degree because most insurance companies scale down the commissions they pay to agents and brokers on larger annuity purchases.

Table X compares annuities worth $10,000 and up. As you can see, administration expenses are lower on larger purchases. The result is more monthly income.

So far, we've discussed only the single-life annuity with no guarantee period. You might wonder who buys this type of annuity.

To be frank, not many people. You shouldn't even consider this type if you are in poor health. And those who wish to control their post-retirement investments should consider a RRIF. However, the single-life annuity with no guarantee might reasonably be bought by a person who doesn't have a family nor a favourite institution or charity to choose as a beneficiary. (This is where the guarantee period comes in, as you'll see later.)

But the life annuity with no guarantee is also an alternative for people who simply want a secure, guaranteed income that requires no management. These annuities are sometimes used in combination with a life insurance policy on the life of the annuitant. You might arrange a life annuity that stops the day you die and buy a life insurance policy that would return money to your beneficiary upon your death.

Joint-And-Last-Survivor Annuities: Reducing Versus Non-Reducing

MALE OR FEMALE, AGE 65
$50,000 RRSP/NO GUARANTEE

	Initial Monthly Income	Monthly Income after Death of One Spouse
100% continuing to survivor	$408.64	$408.64
Reducing by 25% on male's death	425.38	319.04
Reducing by 33% on male's death	431.03	288.79
Reducing by 50% on male's death	443.56	221.78

SOURCE: CANNEX FOR MUTUAL LIFE OF CANADA, JULY 1994

TABLE XI

Since life insurance proceeds are tax-free on death, in some cases this method can provide more money for your estate than an annuity with a guarantee period. We'll go into this concept in more detail later, but for the time being you should recognize that it's important to look at guarantee periods when you choose an annuity. The difference in income between an annuity with a short guarantee and one that stops the day you die can sometimes be trifling, so it often pays to go with the guarantee.

Single-life versus joint-life

The joint-life annuity, a variety of life annuity, provides payments that continue as long as you or your spouse are alive. Also known as the joint-and-last-survivor option, it stops paying upon the death of the surviving spouse.

A number of features are available with the joint-life annuity. One option available at the time of purchase lets you decide whether the full monthly income for both spouses will continue to the survivor, or whether payments will be reduced to half, two-thirds or three-quarters.

For example, Norman buys a joint-life annuity and elects that half the joint-life amount is to continue to his wife, Eileen, upon his death. If he dies first, the monthly payments they received while Norman was alive are cut in half. However, if Eileen dies first, Norman typically continues to get the full monthly cheque without the 50 percent reduction. While most people choose to have the full

Income from a Joint-Life Annuity When One Spouse is Younger

$50,000 RRSP
100% CONTINUING TO SURVIVOR

Ages	Monthly Income
Male 65/female 65 (Mutual Life)	$408.36
Male 65/female 62 (Mutual Life)	400.60
Male 65/female 60 (Mutual Life)	395.24
Male 65/female 50 (Mutual Life)	369.35
Male 65/female 45 (Mutual Life)	360.08

SOURCE: CANNEX, JULY 1994

TABLE XII

payment continued to the survivor, you can get as fancy as you want. For instance, the monthly payment could be reduced upon the death of either spouse, instead of upon the death of the prime annuitant.

Table XI shows the initial monthly payment and the monthly payment in the event of the death of the prime annuitant when full, half, two-thirds and three-quarters payments to the second annuitant are chosen.

As you can see, there is little difference in the initial monthly income while both husband and wife are alive. But there is a substantial difference in income for the survivor after one spouse dies.

Among married couples, the age difference between spouses is on average no greater than three years. In this situation, the difference in monthly payments from a joint-life annuity to a man of sixty-five and a woman of sixty-two is minor. But as Table XII indicates, where there is a larger difference in ages, such as ten years or more, monthly income is reduced to a greater degree.

A life insurance company expects to make payments longer under a joint plan than under a single-life annuity because statistics show that individuals who are married tend to live longer than people who live alone. As a result, joint-life monthly payments are smaller.

When you choose a joint-life annuity, you are in effect buying a life insurance benefit for your spouse. Taking a lesser payment than offered by a single-life annuity makes sense if you're retired or

"Insured" Annuity Versus Joint-Life Annuity

MALE /FEMALE, AGE 65
$100,000 RRSP
40% MARGINAL TAX RATE

	Joint-and-Last Survivor Annuity	Insured Annuity
Monthly income	$809.61	$969.29
Tax	323.84	387.72
After-tax income	485.77	581.57
Monthly cost of life insurance	—	246.60
Net monthly cash flow	485.77	334.97

The income is an average of the highest-paying companies in July 1994. The cost of the insurance is for a male non-smoker.

SOURCE: CANNEX , JULY 1994

TABLE XIII

about to retire. But if you're younger – forty to fifty-five – and you recognize that buying a joint-life annuity is the same as buying life insurance on your own life with your spouse as beneficiary, consider buying real life insurance that will be paid up at your retirement, also with your spouse as beneficiary.

In other words, if there is substantial capital behind you when you retire, whether in the form of paid-up life insurance or other assets, you can afford a little more risk in your choice of an RRSP maturity option. What's more, the insurance proceeds will be tax-free to your spouse, while monthly annuity and RRIF payments are taxable.

Your spouse could simply invest the lump-sum insurance proceeds or buy a type of annuity on which only the interest portion of each payment is taxable. The principal returned with this "prescribed" annuity is tax-free. (For more on prescribed annuities, see chapter 35.)

The technique of arranging a life annuity on your life only, coupled with a life insurance policy, can work in specific situations. Upon death, the commuted value of guaranteed payments remaining under a registered annuity will be paid out and be fully taxable in the estate, as long as there is no spouse or dependent beneficiary, as we'll discuss later.

"Insured" Annuity Versus Single-Life Annuity

MALE, AGE 65 (NON-SMOKER)
$100,000 RRSP
40% MARGINAL TAX RATE

	Life Annuity 15-Year Guarantee	Insured Annuity (Life Only)
Monthly income	$888.07	$969.29
Tax	355.23	387.72
After-tax income	532.84	581.57
Monthly cost of life insurance	—	246.60
Net monthly cash flow	532.84	334.97
Estate value	?	100,000.00

This example assumes that it is desirable to insure 100% of the annuity investment, although it is not necessary for you to do so. Life insurance for any amount less than $100,000 will result in more net monthly cash flow and less for the estate. The cost of the life insurance is based on a male non-smoker.

SOURCE: CANNEX, JULY 1994

TABLE XIV

If one of your objectives is to leave as large an amount as possible when you die, you may find that what's left after tax is less than you were expecting. Not only will Revenue Canada take its share, there may not be much left in the annuity for your family. This would certainly be true if you had a life annuity with a ten-year guarantee and you died in the eighth year. On the other hand, a life insurance policy would leave your family with a known amount of tax-free money, no matter when you die.

Before you decide on an "insured" annuity – that is, a life annuity with no guaranteed payments, plus life insurance – make sure you qualify for the insurance. For people in their sixties, a medical examination is required before a life insurance company will decide whether to offer insurance. This means you must give yourself lead time; it can be six to eight weeks before the policy takes effect.

But don't assume that it will be difficult to get the insurance just because you're in your sixties. Most applicants are approved, and apart from the medical exam it's just a question of how much the premium will be and what kind of policy is best.

Married? Try joint-life

For most married people, the joint-life annuity is clearly superior to a single-life plan. Think of all the widows who have outlived their husbands and who have no incomes from their spouses' pensions. The joint-life annuity solves this problem and provides the peace of mind that comes from knowing that neither of you will outlive your income.

It's a different matter if you're single, widowed or divorced. In this case you must decide whether it is important to leave an estate – to your family or perhaps to your favourite charity. For instance, if you choose a life annuity with a fifteen-year guarantee, you never know exactly what your beneficiary will receive in the form of the commuted value of your annuity. The reason, of course, is that you can't predict when you'll die. If you die after the guarantee period, nothing will be left.

Your alternative is to use an "insured" annuity to maximize what's left for your beneficiary. As you can see from Table XIV, you would arrange for permanent insurance on your life (if you don't already have it), then buy a life annuity with no guarantee. By going this route, the beneficiary is guaranteed the face amount of your insurance policy tax-free. Compare this assured result with not knowing where the beneficiary would stand.

CHAPTER 16

Your Warranty: The Guarantee Period

OF ALL THE OPTIONS YOU must look at when choosing an annuity, one of the most important is the guarantee period. As such, it should be thoroughly understood before you choose to convert your RRSPs to retirement income.

Think of the guarantee period as a warranty, like the one on your car. If your car breaks down after three years under a five-year warranty, the manufacturer will repair it without cost to you. With an annuity, if you die during the guarantee period, your spouse, family, estate or favourite charity will benefit.

As mentioned earlier, "spouse" has been redefined to include a common-law partner with whom you have lived in a conjugal relationship for at least a year. The change means that a qualifying common-law spouse is entitled to the same survivor benefits as a legal spouse, whether the benefits are from a pension plan, a DPSP, an annuity bought with RRSP funds or a RRIF. If you die before your common-law spouse and you have an RRSP, your mate is entitled to a tax-free transfer of RRSP funds to his or her own RRSP.

It's preferable to designate your spouse, whether legal or common-law, as the beneficiary in the contract itself. If the beneficiary is your estate, it is necessary upon your death for your spouse and the legal representative of your estate to file a special form with Revenue Canada. This can result in undue delays and expense.

Minimum payments

Most life annuities – those paid for life, as opposed to those paid to age ninety – include a guaranteed number of payments.

For example, if you buy a single-life annuity with a fifteen-year guarantee and die after five years, your spouse would then continue receiving the same monthly payment for another ten years.

Comparing Single-Life Annuity Options

FEMALE, AGE 65
$50,000 RRSP

Option	Monthly Income
Single life, no guarantee	$437.46
Single life, guaranteed 5 years	433.15
Single life, guaranteed 10 years	422.80
Single life, guaranteed 15 years	408.99
Single life, guaranteed to age 90	377.16

SOURCE: CANNEX FOR CROWN LIFE, JULY 1994

TABLE XV

The longest guarantee with a life annuity is to age ninety, but re-member that payments continue as long as you live – even if it's beyond the guarantee period.

Guarantee periods, which must be chosen at the time you buy an annuity, are commonly five, ten and fifteen years. But a sixty-five-year-old could have a guarantee period of as long as twenty-five years, meaning that if that person died before collecting 300 pay-ments the remaining payments would benefit someone else. The longer the guarantee period, the lower the monthly payments. Table XV shows monthly income from a $50,000 single-life annuity bought by a sixty-five-year-old woman with various guarantees. The concept behind the guarantee period is to be able to leave some money behind if you die prematurely. But is a guarantee necessary with a joint-life annuity? After all, even without a guarantee, the joint-life annuity provides income to you and your spouse no matter how long either of you lives.

No, it's not necessary. But when most people see the small amount of income they would have to give up to add the guarantee, they readily do so. It's better that your family ends up with your money than a life insurance company.

Consider the case of a married couple, each of whom is sixty-seven years old, who use $50,000 in RRSP funds to buy a joint-life annuity. The difference in monthly income between the annuity with no guarantee and one with a fifteen-year guarantee is only $18 a month before tax. So for a small sacrifice in income, you can leave an estate if both of you die before the end of the guarantee period.

Comparing Single-Life and Joint-Life Annuities

MALE OR FEMALE, AGE 71
$50,000 RRSP

Type of Annuity	Monthly Income
Single life (male), no guarantee	$548.01
Single life (male), guaranteed 5 years	531.04
Single life (male), guaranteed 10 years	492.99
Single life (male), guaranteed 15 years	453.17
Single life (male), guaranteed to age 90	426.02
Joint & last survivor, no guarantee	442.54
Joint & last survivor, guaranteed 5 years	441.96
Joint & last survivor, guaranteed 10 years	437.75
Joint & last survivor, guaranteed 15 years	427.42

SOURCE: CANNEX FOR STANDARD LIFE, JULY 1994

TABLE XVI

Here are some tips for considering annuity options:
• Before settling on an annuity with no guarantee, ask for the monthly income on the same type of annuity with five-, ten- and fifteen-year guarantees.
• If you have no children, what about giving up a small amount of income to buy a guarantee that would benefit your church or synagogue, or a favourite charity?
• Joint-life annuities usually require you to give up 10 percent to 15 percent monthly to protect your spouse.
• A life annuity with a guarantee period to age ninety pays only slightly less than a term-certain annuity to ninety but gives you the security of knowing it would still be there if you live longer.
• Some RRIF pay-out alternatives can be designed to function like those of annuities, so be sure you don't buy an annuity without also considering a RRIF in its various forms. More on this later.

CHAPTER 17

Protecting the Younger Spouse

IF YOU ARE A MARRIED breadwinner, you have the responsibility of providing for your spouse in retirement. But what if your spouse is much younger than you – say by ten or twenty years? The age difference could mean that your spouse's need for income may long outlast yours. In this chapter we'll cover some of the alternatives for people in this position who are winding down RRSPs.

The joint-life annuity

If your spouse is not financially independent or if you lack a large life insurance policy that names your younger spouse as beneficiary, you simply have to take reduced income under a joint- life annuity. Even so, you should instruct your annuity broker to shop around, with the age differential in mind. Some life insurance companies offer better deals than others when there is a substantial age difference between spouses.

The single-life annuity

This is an option a married person should choose only if his or her spouse is financially independent and if it is not critical that income from the annuity continue to the spouse. In this case, both husband and wife enjoy the increased income over what a joint-life annuity would provide.

The "insured" life annuity

Anyone who is uncomfortable with the reduction in joint-life annuity income that comes with having a much younger spouse can buy a single-life annuity, which stops paying the day the annuitant dies. Life insurance is then paid tax-free to the surviving spouse to buy a prescribed annuity or to simply invest in any way desired. (For more on prescribed annuities, see Chapter 35.)

However, there are possible pitfalls involved in this strategy. If you don't keep up to date on life insurance premiums, your "insurance" plan will be ineffective. Even if you do keep your insurance in effect, your surviving spouse will have to deal with a large lump sum upon your death – something not everyone is capable of doing. If these conditions worry you, choose a joint-life annuity or a RRIF.

The RRIF

If you have a younger spouse, RRIFs are certainly among the options to consider. We'll go into more detail on RRIFs later, but for now you should be aware that, instead of jumping into an annuity before you feel comfortable with one, you can use a RRIF temporarily to create income for you and your spouse. You can structure the payments of a RRIF according to the age of the younger spouse, then choose the amount of current income you'll need. Upon the death of the first spouse, the survivor can continue with the RRIF or change to a single-life annuity. If we assume there has been no erosion of capital at this point, the single-life annuity would pay more than a joint-life plan would have.

Which to choose?

Which of these methods should you choose to protect your younger spouse? That depends not only on your spouse's age, but on your and your spouse's other financial resources, your ability to manage money and your health. Have your annuity/RRIF broker produce a detailed comparison of your alternatives and how they relate to your circumstances.

CHAPTER 18

Variations on a Theme

WHEN YOU BOUGHT YOUR last car you probably agonized over the many options available: colour, air conditioning, engine type and a host of other features. Well, annuities, like cars, also come in a variety of models. And like cars, there are several options to choose from in each category. Let's look at them.

Cashable annuities

You've likely heard that choosing an annuity is an irrevocable decision. But when the federal government liberalized rules governing RRIFs and annuities in 1986, it also allowed companies to offer annuities that can be cashed in or "commuted."

To date, only a few companies have marketed annuities that are specifically designed with the cashing-in option. However, most financial institutions offering annuities will consider letting you cash a term-certain-to-ninety annuity because it is a simple matter to calculate the commuted value. Determining the value of a life annuity, on the other hand, is a much more difficult proposition.

Why would anyone want to cash an annuity? Some reasons that come to mind are poor health, higher interest rates than when the annuity was purchased, the need for cash and the desire to switch to a RRIF.

Let's look at three approaches to the cashable annuity.

Insurance giant Sun Life Assurance Co. of Canada offers an annuity that gives purchasers the option of cashing in five years from the date of purchase and at five-year intervals after that. This flexibility comes at a price. For example, in July 1994, a sixty-five-year-old man could use a $100,000 RRSP to buy a normal, non-cashable life annuity with a fifteen-year guarantee that would provide monthly income of $881.18. The same capital would produce $848.06 a month with Sun Life's cashable annuity, 3.75 percent less.

A second product, from NN Life Insurance Co. of Canada (formerly Mony Life Insurance Co. of Canada), is called the Annuity Plus. It's a term-certain annuity to age ninety, but with some interesting twists. The plan is promoted as having "the guarantee of an annuity, the performance of a RRIF." At three-year or five-year intervals from the date of purchase, various things can happen:

• You can choose to renew the plan for another three or five years, but with higher payments.

• If interest rates have fallen dramatically, you are guaranteed at least the same payments for the next three or five years that you have had for the previous three or five years.

• You can take out cash, subject to tax being withheld by the company to satisfy government requirements.

• You can convert the Annuity Plus at no cost to an NN single-life or joint-life annuity.

• You can switch to another company's annuity or RRIF.

As is the case with Sun Life's cashable annuity, you pay for the flexibility of the NN Life plan. You would receive about 85 percent of what you could get by going with a plain-vanilla term-to-ninety annuity.

The most liberal approach is that of Security Life Insurance Corp., which allows you to cash any of its regular annuities at any time. It should be noted, however, that you are prevented by law from cashing annuities bought with money from pension funds or "locked-in" RRSPs. (With these proceeds you do not have the RRIF as an option. You must use locked-in pension proceeds for an annuity or life income fund (LIF).

Security Life doesn't charge for cashing an annuity, but the amount you get is subject to a "market value adjustment." If interest rates are higher than when you bought the annuity, you will get a lower amount than if interest rates had remained static. On the other hand, you win if interest rates have gone down because the cash value will be higher.

Security Life will even let you cash a life annuity. The cash value will equal the present value of any remaining payments under the guarantee period, plus 75 percent of the present value of the estimated payments from the end of the guarantee period to life expectancy (based on your age at the time of purchase).

There is one important caveat, however. There must have been no "life-threatening change" in your health since you bought the

Indexed Annuities

MALE OR FEMALE, AGE 60
$50,000 RRSP
JOINT AND LAST SURVIVOR, GUARANTEED 15 YEARS

| Option | Monthly Income | | | |
	Year 1	Year 5	Year 10	Year 20
Level	376.10	376.10	376.10	376.10
4% indexing	249.94	304.10	369.98	547.67
Indexed to 60% of CPI*	246.84	277.92	312.91	396.66
Fully indexed to CPI*	219.39	266.93	324.76	480.72

* Monthly incomes for the partially and fully indexed options assume the Consumer Price Index (CPI) increases 4% annually. The incomes beyond year one for both alternatives are not guaranteed; the figures are calculated based upon the previous year's increase in the CPI.

SOURCE: STANDARD LIFE ASSURANCE COMPANY, JULY 1994

TABLE XVII

annuity. The company would require a letter to that effect from your doctor.

If there has been such a change in health, the cash value would amount to the present value of the remaining payments under the guarantee period. But if you live beyond the guarantee period, the company would resume your monthly payments at the original amount and continue them for life.

Indexing annuities for inflation

Most payments from the types of annuities we've already discussed can be indexed to provide protection from inflation. Indeed, long-term benefits from indexing can be significant – but you have to sacrifice current income. You can choose from these indexing formulas, although no one company offers them all:

• Indexing guaranteed at 4 percent, compounded annually on each anniversary of your first monthly annuity payment.

• Annual indexing based on a rate equal to three percentage points less than the average yield from federal government ninety-day treasury bills for each previous quarter before the anniversary date of your annuity.

• Annual indexing of 60 percent of the increase in the Consumer Price Index over the previous calendar year.

• Annual indexing fully reflecting the increase in the CPI over the previous calendar year.

Depending on which indexing formula you choose, you'll have to take initial payments of 33 percent to almost 45 percent less than with a level-payment annuity purchased with the same amount of money.

Table XVII shows monthly incomes for years one, five, ten and twenty that would be paid out by a joint-and-last-survivor annuity bought with a $50,000 RRSP and guaranteed for fifteen years. In this case, the husband and wife are both sixty.

While most life insurance companies offer 4 percent guaranteed indexing, there is a wide spread in annuity payments. As for other forms of indexing, you're more restricted by what is available "off the shelf." For indexing linked to the Consumer Price Index, Standard Life Assurance Co. is the major player. Other companies will occasionally quote on this form of indexing if requested.

Whatever you do, don't choose an indexed pension in isolation. Consider what investments and pensions you have and whether they are likely to increase with inflation.

As we noted in earlier chapters, CPP retirement benefits and OAS are fully indexed to inflation. But employer pensions outside the public sector are usually not. So if you have a non-indexed pension, you will want to consider a RRIF or an indexed annuity, especially if you're in good health.

Some people like the comfort of having retirement income that increases each year. Others prefer to receive the income up front and take care of inflation themselves, or they want to control their money through a RRIF with escalating withdrawals. The best solution is the one that lets you sleep soundly.

Deferred annuities

So far, the annuities we've looked at begin payments from the date of purchase. If you prefer, however, you can buy a deferred annuity, with payments beginning years down the road – although by law, the latest you can defer the start of monthly payments is January of your seventy-second year.

There are good reasons to defer payments. First, you might not need income right away, but you might want to lock in your money at current interest rates. Second, you might be close to retirement and worried that interest rates will decline, so you could decide to

---

Deferring Your First Annuity Payment

MALE OR FEMALE, AGE 65
$50,000 RRSP
JOINT AND LAST SURVIVOR, 15-YEAR GUARANTEE
(100% TO SURVIVOR)

Starting Date	Monthly Income
1 month after purchase (immediate)	$405.48
3 months after purchase	411.97
6 months after purchase	422.36
12 months after purchase	444.80
24 months after purchase	491.89
60 months after purchase	662.59

SOURCE: CANNEX FOR MUTUAL LIFE OF CANADA, JULY 1994

TABLE XVIII

buy now. And third, you might have turned seventy-one but want to shelter income in the current tax year.

Deferred annuities can be set up to start anywhere from a few months to ten years from purchase. The longer you're prepared to wait, the greater the income you will receive. That's because the money is generating interest without any payments.

Table XVIII, based on a $50,000 RRSP, shows how payments can be increased by deferring their starting date.

Canada Life, Imperial Life, Great-West Life and Manulife Financial offer a unique deferred annuity that can be bought with either RRSP or company pension proceeds. You can elect five optional starting dates within ten years or the end of the year when you reach seventy-one, whichever comes first. As each option date rolls around, you can trigger the start of monthly income or defer your decision until the next option date. The longer you wait, the greater the income guaranteed in the contract.

Let's take the example of a sixty-two-year-old man who buys a Canada Life deferred annuity with optional starting dates coinciding with his sixty-fourth, sixty-fifth, sixty-sixth and sixty-eighth birthdays, as well as the end of the year in which he reaches seventy-one. Table XIX shows the monthly payments he would receive starting on each date, if we assume he has a $50,000 joint-life annuity with fifteen years of guaranteed payments.

Canada Life's "Optional Income Date"

DEFERRED ANNUITY MALE OR FEMALE, AGE 62
$50,000 RRSP
JOINT AND LAST SURVIVOR
15-YEAR GUARANTEE (100% TO SURVIVOR)

Optional starting date (male's birth-date)	Monthly Income
64th	$452.87
65th	498.90
66th	549.75
68th	664.72
71st	876.14

SOURCE: CANADA LIFE ASSURANCE CO., JULY 1994

TABLE XIX

Before choosing a deferred annuity, consider the alternative of simply leaving your RRSP intact (if you're under seventy-one) and arranging the annuity later. The risk, of course, is that you don't know where interest rates will be when you eventually make your move.

Annuity incomes vary according to long-term bond rates. Because long-term bond rates are generally higher than rates for GICs – and assuming annuity rates remain unchanged – you will generally receive more income by choosing a deferred annuity than you would by leaving the money in an RRSP consisting of one-year to five-year GICs. But there is always the possibility that interest rates will rise just when you think they'll fall. So a deferred annuity can be risky if you're buying now because you are convinced rates won't move up. Once you buy the annuity you can't accelerate the starting date if you need the income sooner.

Impaired annuities

If you have a serious health problem, your life expectancy is reduced. As a result, for the purpose of annuities, life insurance companies are willing to treat you as if you're older than you are. That leads to higher monthly payments – one of the few financial rewards of ill health.

It is not necessary to be critically ill. A history of heart ailments, cancer, high blood pressure, strokes or diabetes may qualify you for an impaired annuity. There can be a wide variation in the amount of extra money insurance companies will offer the same person, and the maturity option you choose also affects the equation. One company might act as if a sixty-five-year-old were seventy; another might base its calculation on the life expectancy of a seventy-five-year-old. An annuity/RRIF broker can find you the best deal.

The impaired option is available only with life or joint-life annuities. That's because there must be an element of mortality that can be improved upon. This is not the case with a term-to-ninety annuity or a RRIF.

If your health is poor and you were leaning toward a term-certain annuity or a RRIF, you might consider an impaired annuity simply because it's too good a deal to refuse. You don't need a medical examination to qualify; a letter from your doctor detailing your current medical condition, past history and continuing treatment is adequate.

If you qualify for an impaired annuity, it's important to choose the right options to protect your spouse. As with other annuity and RRIF choices, this may mean settling for less than you would otherwise. Factors to consider besides your health are your spouse's health, inflation protection, whether you want to leave an estate and what income-producing assets you have apart from your RRSP and pension.

Poor health can also work to your financial advantage with an employer pension. Ask your employer's benefits officer. However, you can't get an impaired annuity or similar treatment with a pension after you start receiving the income. There's no retroactivity; if there's even a possibility that you might qualify, find out beforehand.

Applying for an impaired annuity, or equivalent pension treatment, is a no-lose situation. If you're turned down, you'll find yourself in the same position as everyone else your age; if not, your retirement income will be larger than expected.

CHAPTER 19

Interest Rates and Your Retirement Income

AS INSURANCE COMPANY
actuaries calculate annuity payments they take into account life expectancy, the company's expenses and interest rates. Of the three, interest rates are the most important. If you buy an annuity when interest rates are 12 percent, you will receive much higher income than you would if you purchase during a period of 8 percent rates.

As a result of this dependence on interest levels, annuities change frequently. Most life insurance companies will decide on their annuity rates and, providing the interest rate environment is not volatile, will stay with them for a few weeks.

From the buyer's viewpoint, the purchase of an annuity is usually an irrevocable decision. You lock in prevailing interest rates at the time of purchase and there's no way to change your mind. Insurance companies are adamant on this point because they match their financial obligation to you with the purchase of long-term bonds, usually in the ten- to twenty-year range.

Details of current annuity incomes can be found in the pages of many daily newspapers. You'll notice that amounts go up and down from month to month, reflecting changes in bond yields.

The Government of Canada average bond yield from 1978 to 1993 for bonds of ten-year terms and longer varied from 7.5 percent to 15.22 percent. Obviously, if you had bought an annuity in 1981, when rates were at their peak, you would be receiving much more income than you would had you purchased the annuity at another time.

Table XX shows what an annuity bought with a $50,000 RRSP would produce for a man aged sixty-five under various interest-rate assumptions. As a rule of thumb, a one-percentage-point change in long-term interest rates means a difference of 6 percent to 7 percent in the monthly income you would receive, regardless of the size of your investment. Someone considering the purchase of an annuity

Comparing Annuity Incomes at Various Interest Rates

MALE, AGE 65
$50,000 RRSP
LIFE ANNUITY
15-YEAR GUARANTEE

Interest Rate	Monthly Annuity Income
6%	$363.91
8%	420.85
9%	450.04
10%	479.99
11%	510.74
12%	542.03
14%	604.22

Income starts one month after purchase. Once you purchase an annuity, the income is guaranteed based on interest rates in effect at the time of purchase. Other factors which have an impact on annuity incomes are life expectancy and expenses of the annuity company.

TABLE XX

that would produce $1,000 a month of income would find that if interest rates rose by one percentage point before purchase, monthly income would increase to about $1,070.

Everyone considering annuities would like to buy when interest rates are at a peak. Deciding when that peak has arrived is not an easy task. Economists and other financial experts usually disagree, leaving hindsight as the only true measure.

For example, in 1981 and 1982, when short-term interest rates were in the high teens and annuity incomes were based on yields of 14 percent to 15 percent, many people bought annuities to lock in the high rates. Others thought interest rates were headed higher, so they put off their decision. As it turned out, annuity rates were at this level for about fourteen months before money costs eased.

Of course, there is a downside to the interest-rate equation: you don't want to wait until you must make your annuity/RRIF decision (remember, your RRSPs must be dealt with by December 31 of the year in which you turn seventy-one) and find that interest rates are low.

RRIFs to the rescue

Fortunately, this isn't as great a problem as it was in the past. Under today's rules, if interest rates are down, you can buy a short-term investment through a RRIF and hope interest rates rise to the point where you would be comfortable buying an annuity. You can also consider the following options:

• You could buy a series of annuities over a period of years to average out interest rates.

• If you feel rates are reasonably high, you could buy a deferred annuity, lock in today's interest rates and arrange for your annuity payments to start no later than the end of the year in which you turn seventy-one.

• You could choose a "prepaid" RRIF (see Chapter 31), again to lock in today's interest rates, and start your payments at a later date.

• You could postpone your decision, hoping interest rates will rise.

The last two strategies assume that you don't need income today. However, at retirement most people need as much income as they can get their hands on.

CHAPTER 20

Annuities: What's Left for Your Estate?

MOST PEOPLE SHOPPING FOR annuities are concerned about what will be left when they die, in part owing to a common misconception that everything that remains ends up in a life insurance company's coffers. This just isn't so.

While an annuity will likely leave a lower estate value than a RRIF bought with the same amount of RRSP funds, it can still provide for money to be left to your estate, family or a charitable organization — even if you live close to age ninety.

In earlier chapters we discussed the importance of a guarantee period as part of your annuity. Let's review the basic rules governing what happens when you die:

• If you arrange a single-life annuity with a guarantee period, and your spouse survives you, your spouse will be paid the same monthly income until the end of the guarantee period. However, if you die after the guarantee period, nothing is left.

• With a joint-and-last-survivor annuity, payments of either the same amount or a reduced amount will continue to your spouse, depending on what you arranged at the time of purchase. A guarantee period on a joint-life annuity serves the purpose of leaving money for your family or estate should both you and your spouse die before receiving the minimum number of guaranteed payments.

• A term-certain annuity provides for payments to continue to your ninetieth year. If you die before then, your spouse continues to collect until the year in which you would have turned ninety (or the annuity could be based on the younger spouse's age ninety). If you are survived by a husband or wife and have structured your annuity accordingly, the monthly payments will continue to your spouse without interruption if you die first.

Following the death of both spouses – or your death if you're single, widowed or divorced – your annuity is effectively cashed. Anything left under a guarantee – or with a term-certain annuity, the amount that was to be paid to your or your spouse's ninetieth year – is commuted and the "present value" of the remaining payments is paid. The government gets a share of this through your last income tax bill.

This means the amount the insurance company has set aside to provide for the remaining guaranteed payments is paid to your estate or named beneficiaries. How much your beneficiaries or estate receive will depend on four factors: where interest rates are at the time you die; how many payments are left in the guarantee period; the amount of these payments; and the level of interest rates at the time of your death compared with rates when you bought the annuity. In other words, if you have a single-life annuity with a ten-year guarantee period and you die after five years, the life insurance company doesn't simply pay the sum of the remaining five years of payments to your estate or beneficiaries.

Present value varies

Calculation of the present value depends on a formula in the annuity contract or the life insurance company's current practice.

Most companies use a commutation rate that is the greater of the interest rate at the time of death and the interest-rate assumption in your annuity contract. This means you can't determine how much will be available to your estate.

To demonstrate how this complex calculation works, let's take the case of a single person who purchases a $500 a month life annuity with a ten-year guarantee and dies after five years. Normally, this person would have collected at least $6,000 a year for the next five years – and beyond that if he was still living. So you might assume that since there were at least five years of payments left in the guarantee, the beneficiaries would collect $30,000 (five times $6,000). In fact, the beneficiaries would collect the commuted value of about $24,400, assuming an 8.75 percent interest rate at the time of death. If interest rates were higher, the beneficiaries would receive less. If interest rates were lower, they would receive more.

Keep in mind, however, that for most companies the interest rate used in commuting the remaining payments will never be less than the interest assumption in the annuity contract. It could be higher;

some companies use either the rate in the annuity contract or current interest rates, whichever is higher.

Some advice: assuming you're happy with annuities and want the guaranteed income while you're living, as well as the other advantages of annuities, you'll have to decide to what degree you want your estate to benefit if you die before the end of the guarantee period. Since you don't know when you're going to die, you must decide whether to sacrifice current income to build an estate.

The only way to favour your estate is to take a longer guarantee period, which means more will be left over. If you die after five years of receiving annuity payments, an annuity with a fifteen-year guarantee will leave more than an annuity with a ten-year guarantee. And an annuity with a guarantee to age ninety will leave more than any other kind of life annuity. In no circumstances is there anything left for your estate if you outlive the guarantee period or live beyond age ninety.

It's not only the commuted value that counts in working out estate values. This income will be taxable if you're single, widowed or divorced when you die. In the example above, the estate of the deceased taxpayer would have to include the $24,400 in income for the year of death.

Relief for beneficiaries

There is some tax relief if the beneficiaries include children or grandchildren who are considered dependents. In this case, the full amount can be transferred as a lump sum to a child. The dependent child or grandchild has the option to spread the tax by purchasing a special annuity paying out equal annual installments until the child reaches age eighteen.

No dollar limit applies if the child or grandchild is a dependent because of physical or mental impairment. In this situation, the recipient can transfer the annuity proceeds tax-free into an RRSP or use the money to buy an annuity or RRIF.

If your beneficiary is not a spouse nor a dependent child or grandchild, the commuted value of the annuity will be taxable as income on your final tax return.

CHAPTER 21

RRIFs: The Basics

THE RRIF HAS BEEN AROUND since 1978 but until significant changes were made in 1986 it was not a popular retirement option.

In its original form, the RRIF was disliked by the majority of Canadians because it paid less in the initial years of retirement than an annuity bought with identical RRSP proceeds. In fact, its appeal was largely limited to higher-income retirees looking to defer tax.

An optional RRIF formula that was introduced in 1983 offered somewhat higher payments in early years, but this meant lower payments later. Canadians largely ignored this RRIF variation as well.

However, changes that took effect in December 1986 turned this ugly duckling of retirement options into a swan. Pensioners were suddenly allowed much more flexibility and control over retirement income. To provide you with increased options during your retirement years, an extension to the payout schedule for RRIFs was announced in the February 1992 federal budget. This permits withdrawals over your lifetime (or the lifetime of your spouse, if married) rather than to age ninety as was previously the case. It is effective for all RRIFs to which funds are transferred after 1992.

Let's look first at the original RRIF and then go into the changes that have made it the most popular of retirement income options.

Start with RRSP proceeds

Like an annuity, a RRIF is bought with RRSP proceeds. The annuity or RRIF purchase must take place by the end of the year in which you reach age seventy-one. Current RRIF rules allow the fund – that is, the principal amount you contribute, plus earnings over the years – to last over your lifetime, even if you live beyond age 100. Minimum withdrawals are required each year. More details on this in the next chapter.

In rewriting the RRIF rules in 1986, the government made a major change by allowing RRIF holders to withdraw any amount each year, as long as they withdrew at least the minimum. This meant that you could either take out all your money over a shorter time period or take it out slowly, keeping the RRIF intact until a later age.

Other new rules contributing to the RRIF's greater flexibility and the purchaser's greater control over his or her money include the following:

- You can have more than one RRIF. Before this change, your only alternative if you were unhappy with the institution that issued your plan was to transfer it to another company. You weren't allowed to have more than one RRIF.
- Payments can start at any time during the year you buy the RRIF and no later than the end of the calendar year following purchase.
- You're allowed to cash in, or commute, an annuity and transfer the proceeds tax-free to a RRIF. You can go the other way and make a tax-free transfer from a RRIF to an annuity. More on this later.
- As with annuities, you can now set up a RRIF before age sixty, something you couldn't do before the 1986 changes.

In effect, you can design your own pension by using a RRIF. But you must be aware than anything removed from your plan is fully taxable as pension income.

Why choose a RRIF?

Why consider RRIFs? Because they're the most flexible retirement income option. They're for people who want to keep pace with inflation, defer taxes and provide an estate. A RRIF can be a continuation of your RRSP. You can draw minimum payments so that the fund continues to grow for many years or you can take more money out. But you must keep in mind that withdrawals reduce your income later in life. If you're looking for flexibility and control over your investments, you should consider buying a RRIF, or RRIFs, with some or all of your RRSP. But before doing so, make sure you have a firm handle on your income needs and understand how the RRIF can help you in later years.

As you'll see later, you may have to pay a price for the RRIF's flexibility. On the other hand a RRIF, if handled carefully, can be your most valuable source of retirement income.

CHAPTER 22

Variety Is the Spice of RRIFs

A RRIF IS AN EXTREMELY flexible retirement option. It allows you not only to control how your money will be invested, but how your payments will work as well. Let's look at the six common RRIF payment alternatives:

- The minimum payments permitted by law;
- "Smoothed" payments;
- Interest-only payments;
- Level payments;
- Indexed payments that rise by a certain percentage each year;
- Payments for a fixed term.

Minimum payments

Choosing a RRIF with minimum payments is like continuing an RRSP as a tax shelter, having to make periodic withdrawals instead of contributions. Table XXI shows the minimum monthly RRIF payments each year to age 100 based on a $50,000 investment. In this example, and in the others to follow, we have assumed that on December 1st you transfer $50,000 from an RRSP to a RRIF earning 8 percent for its entire existence.

You'll see that in this case, the original capital increases and does not drop below $50,000 until age eighty-nine. This will, of course, vary with the investment return. Note that at 8 percent the plan value peaks at age seventy-five. The income figures are based on monthly withdrawals, although you may choose annual, quarterly or semi-annual payments instead.

This type of plan is suitable for someone who is concerned about inflation and is looking to enhance retirement income. It is also for those who have enough other retirement income and would like to defer income tax, and for those who want to start with minimum payments and increase them later.

The Lifetime RRIF

$50,000 INVESTMENT
MALE OR FEMALE, AGE 65
DEPOSIT DATE: DECEMBER 1
FIRST MONTHLY PAYMENT: JANUARY 1

Age	Monthly Payments	Fund Value Jan. 1	Age	Monthly Payments	Fund Value Jan.1
66	$167.76	$50,328	84	$459.49	$57,556
67	181.44	52,254	85	466.79	56,410
68	196.25	54,164	86	474.15	55,080
69	212.28	56,041	87	481.52	53,552
70	229.63	57,867	88	489.17	51,810
71	248.43	59,622	89	496.66	49,832
72	376.89	61,283	90	504.19	47,602
73	383.15	61,468	91	511.89	45,100
74	389.56	61,590	92	519.25	42,301
75	396.05	61,642	93	526.41	39,187
76	403.07	61,616	94	533.61	35,733
77	409.49	61,501	95	531.88	31,913
78	416.30	61,296	96	463.48	27,809
79	423.36	60,989	97	403.88	24,233
80	430.55	60,569	98	351.94	21,117
81	437.69	60,026	99	306.68	18,401
82	444.63	59,350	100	267.25	16,035
83	452.17	58,533			

Total payments: $167,843.28
This stream of income assumes an interest rate of 8 percent compounded annually after each payment is withdrawn. The minimum payment is based on the value of the RRIF at December 31 each year.

TABLE XXI

The lifetime payment RRIF is the version that was introduced in 1992. The RRIF illustrated in Table XXI, with monthly payments starting one month after the plan is set up, allows for maximum growth in fund value. If you opt for the convenience of monthly payments, they will be 1/12 of the minimum annual withdrawal, but your fund value will not grow as large because you're taking out money sooner.

Minimum RRIF Withdrawals*

Age	Old	New	Age	Old	New
71	5.26%	7.38%	86	25.00%	10.79%
72	5.56	7.48	87	33.33	11.33
73	5.88	7.59	88	50.00	11.96
74	6.25	7.71	89	100.00	12.71
75	6.67	7.85	90	—	13.62
76	7.14	7.99	91	—	14.73
77	7.69	8.15	92	—	16.12
78	8.33	8.33	93	—	17.92
79	9.09	8.53	94	—	20.00
80	10.00	8.75	95	—	20.00
81	11.11	8.99	96	—	20.00
82	12.50	9.27	97	—	20.00
83	14.29	9.58	98	—	20.00
84	16.67	9.93	99	—	20.00
85	20.00	10.330	100	—	20.00

*Expressed as a percentage of RRIF assets.

TABLE XXII

Under the revised rules, it's important to recognize that the new schedule only applies to minimum withdrawals. If you are under age seventy-one, minimum withdrawals are based on the value of your RRIF at the end of each calendar year divided by the number of years until age ninety. A seventy-year-old with $50,000 has to draw a minimum of 1/20th in year one. Under the revised rules minimum withdrawals will be determined as a percentage of RRIF assets, again using a year-end value. From Table XXII you can see that in year one this would amount to 7.38 percent for a seventy-one year old. Therefore, unless your underlying RRIF investments earn more than 7 or 8 percent your plan value will decrease after age seventy-one.

Under the new rules minimum payments in the early years are higher than previously allowed, but lower after age seventy-eight. As a result, you will not be able to defer as much tax. Secondly, once you reach age ninety-four, you must withdraw 20 percent of the declining balance in your fund each year. The effect of this new

Qualifying RRIF: Pre-1993
Minimum Monthly Payments

$50,000 INVESTMENT
MALE OR FEMALE, AGE 65
DEPOSIT DATE: DECEMBER 1
FIRST MONTHLY PAYMENT: JANUARY 1

Age	Monthly Payments	Fund Value January 1	Age	Monthly Payments	Fund Value January 1
66	$167.76	$50,328	84	507.95	$63,627
67	181.44	52,254	85	516.02	62,359
68	196.25	54.164	86	524.16	60,889
69	212.28	56,041	87	532.31	59,200
70	229.63	57,867	88	540.76	57,274
71	248.43	59,622	89	549.04	55,088
72	268.78	61,283	90	557.36	52,623
73	290.84	62,821	91	565.87	49,857
74	314.74	64,207	92	574.02	46,763
75	340.65	65,404	93	581.93	43,320
76	368.74	66,373	94	589.89	39,502
77	399.21	67,068	95	587.98	35,279
78	432.29	67,437	96	512.37	30,742
79	468.02	67,421	97	446.47	26,788
80	475.95	66,957	98	389.06	23,344
81	483.85	66,357	99	339.03	20,342
82	491.52	65,609	100	295.43	17,726
83	499.86	64,706			

This stream of income assumes an 8 percent annual compound yield.
Total payments to age 100 are $176,158.67 but can continue beyond
that age.

TABLE XXIII

schedule is to level out your payments more so than under the pre-
1993 rules.

The post-1992 minimum rules do not affect you until you reach
age seventy-one. If you have a RRIF set up before 1993, the "old"
minimum withdrawal requirements will apply up to age seventy-
seven. At age seventy-eight, the new rules take over and the lower
minimums as shown in the table will apply. A RRIF arranged prior

to 1993 is now known as a "qualifying" RRIF (refer to table XXIII for an example).

Under a qualifying RRIF you can defer more tax than with the lifetime RRIF since minimum payments are lower from age seventy-one to seventy-seven. If tax deferral is your objective, be certain not to add new money to a qualifying RRIF by means of a RRSP or RRIF transfer since this taints the RRIF and subjects it to the post-1992 rules.

The payment schedule you choose also affects the interest you earn on your RRIF. Most trust companies, banks, credit unions and some life insurance companies quote a reduced interest rate – usually half a percentage point less – if you choose monthly payments. For example, you might be offered 8 percent on an annual basis or 7.5 percent on a monthly basis. Taking the 8 percent means you would receive your first cheque one year after you set up your RRIF.

On the other hand, most life insurance companies, some trust companies and credit unions advertise an annual compound yield that remains in effect until your term deposit matures. This means the interest credited to your RRIF will compound annually after each payment is withdrawn, whether the withdrawals are monthly or annual.

While you could suffer a financial penalty by taking your payments monthly, you will have the use of the funds sooner. Compare computer printouts from different companies to be sure you get the most for your money. The key figures are how much you receive and what your fund value is at any time. If you're comfortable with your income, consider starting with minimum payments and switching to one of the other options later.

"Smoothed" payments

Recognizing that the old minimum payment formula was unpopular, the federal government introduced an optional formula in 1983, the so-called 6 percent smoothing factor, that allowed RRIF holders to withdraw more in early retirement years in return for smaller increases later. Although the withdrawal ceiling has since been removed, some people like the smoothing approach. Table XXIV shows the results of the smoothing technique with a payout to age ninety. Even with the removal of the age ninety ending date for RRIFs, this option is still available from many financial institutions, particularly life insurance companies.

RRIF 6 Percent Smoothing: Age-Ninety Payout

$50,000 INVESTMENT
MALE OR FEMALE, AGE 65
DEPOSIT DATE: DECEMBER 1
FIRST MONTHLY PAYMENT: JANUARY 1

Age	Monthly Payments	Fund Value January 1	Age	Monthly Payments	Fund Value January1
66	$309.51	$50,328	79	$411.68	$43,903
67	316.21	50,480	80	421.27	42,262
68	323.08	50,561	81	431.22	40,371
69	330.11	50,562	82	441.57	38,203
70	337.32	50,476	83	452.38	35,733
71	344.71	50,292	84	463.74	32,929
72	352.29	50,001	85	475.79	29,760
73	360.07	49,592	86	488.71	26,185
74	368.07	49,052	87	502.85	22,164
75	376.28	48,370	88	518.90	17,643
76	384.73	47,530	89	538.57	12,560
77	393.44	46,517	90	568.66	6,824
78	402.41	45,314			

Final withdrawal: $252.50
Total payments: $124,015.40
This stream of income assumes an 8 percent interest rate compounded annually after each payment is withdrawn.

TABLE XXIV

The often misunderstood 6 percent smoothing formula is an actuarial calculation, not a simple 6 percent increase in RRIF payments each year. It involves what are known as "annuity due factors" that give you the present value of $1 paid out for the number of years until age ninety, assuming a certain interest return.

Let's look at the example in Table XXIV. In this case, $13.55036 is the amount that would have to be set aside today to support payments of $1 a year for twenty-five years when earning 6 percent interest. To determine the payment schedule starting with the first full calendar year (age sixty-six), divide $13.55036 into the value of the RRIF on December 31 ($50,328). This indicates that the total withdrawal in the first full calendar year must be $3,714.14, or $309.51 a month, as shown in the table.

Despite the 6 percent smoothing label, many companies allow a range of smoothing factors. A choice of 0 percent to 6 percent (0 percent smoothing is the minimum payment formula) is common, with some companies offering factors of up to 9 percent or more.

Some even allow a smoothing factor as high as the interest rate on your investment. The higher the smoothing factor, the more income you will receive in the early years and the faster your RRIF will be depleted. In other words, you smooth out your payments. However, in the case of all the smoothing factors described, your RRIF will not run out until the year you turn ninety. And even with higher smoothing factors, payments in later years still increase, but at a lesser rate.

The best way to see how a particular payment scheme works is to ask the financial institution or your financial advisor for a computer printout demonstrating the payments over the life of the RRIF.

Interest-only payments

When the RRIF withdrawal ceiling was lifted, many creative formulas emerged. Among these is a technique that leaves the principal of your investment intact while you withdraw only the interest.

Under this system, shown in Table XXV, more than the minimum requirement is taken out in the early years by withdrawing the exact amount of interest earned. In this case, the monthly withdrawal remains constant until your seventy-eighth year, when the required minimum withdrawal rises above $321.68. You should also note that with an interest-only RRIF, which appeals mainly to people who dislike annuities, there is no growth of capital. This illustrates an age-100 payout on an interest-only basis.

Level payments

With a level-payment RRIF, illustrated in Table XXVI, you choose to withdraw the same amount each month through to age ninety. This would be an alternative to using a term-certain-to-age-ninety annuity. In our example, the level payment for the full term of the RRIF is $376.69 a month. Contrast this with an annuity which would provide $402.52 to age ninety, or $402 to $453 for life (or joint life, depending on the option chosen).

RRIF Interest-Only Payments: Age-100 Payout

$50,000 INVESTMENT
MALE OR FEMALE, AGE 65
DEPOSIT DATE: DECEMBER 1
FIRST MONTHLY PAYMENT: JANUARY 1

Age	Monthly Payments	Fund Value	Age	Monthly Payments	Fund Value
66	$321.68	$50,328	84	$379.10*	$47,486
67	321.68	50,328	85	385.12*	46,540
68	321.68	50,328	86	391.19*	45,443
69	321.68	50,328	87	397.27*	44,182
70	321.68	50,328	88	403.58*	42,745
71	321.68	50,328	89	409.76*	41,113
72	321.68	50,329	90	415.97*	39,274
73	321.68	50,329	91	422.32*	37,209
74	321.68	50,329	92	428.40*	34,900
75	321.68	50,329	93	434.30*	32,330
76	321.68	50,329	94	440.25*	29,481
77	321.68	50,329	95	438.82*	26,329
78	322.63*	50,330	96	382.39*	22,944
79	349.29*	50,318	97	333.22*	19,993
80	355.22*	49,972	98	290.36*	17,422
81	361.11*	49,524	99	253.02*	15,181
82	366.84*	49,966	100	220.49*	13,229
83	373.05*	48,292			

*Point at which minimum payments exceed interest only.
Assumes 8 percent annual compound yield. Payments may continue beyond age ninety.

TABLE XXV

So what's the difference between this type of RRIF and a term-certain annuity to age ninety? As far as income goes, there is little. But with the term-certain annuity, you hand over your money and never again have any control over your funds. The RRIF lets you change your mind at any time and pick another payment formula, subject to investment restrictions.

However, if you invest your RRIF for five-year periods, interest rates will change at renewal. As a result, it will be difficult to duplicate the term-certain annuity's guaranteed rate. You might have to

RRIF Level Payments: Age-Ninety Payout

$50,000 INVESTMENT
MALE OR FEMALE, AGE 65
DEPOSIT DATE: DECEMBER 1
FIRST MONTHLY PAYMENT: JANUARY 1

Age	Monthly Payment	Fund Value Jan. 1	Age	Monthly Payment	Fund Value Jan. 1
66	$376.69	$50,328	79	$376.69	$35,530
67	376.69	49,639	80	376.69	33,658
68	376.69	48,896	81	376.69	31,636
69	376.69	48,093	82	376.69	29,452
70	376.69	47,226	83	376.69	27,094
71	376.69	46,289	84	376.69	24,547
72	376.69	45,278	85	376.69	21,796
73	376.69	44,185	86	376.69	18,825
74	376.69	43,006	87	376.69	15,616
75	376.69	41,731	88	376.69	12,151
76	376.69	40,355	89	376.69	8,408
77	376.69	38,869	90	376.69	4,366
78	376.69	37,264			

Total payments: $113,007.02
This stream of income assumes an 8 percent interest rate compounded annually after each payment is withdrawn.

TABLE XXVI

adjust RRIF withdrawals every five years to ensure that your money lasts as long as an annuity, particularly if interest rates are down at renewal. On the other hand, you can choose a guaranteed interest rate for the full term of the RRIF. Such long-term RRIFs are readily available through life insurance companies.

Indexed payments

Rather than settling for level payments, you can opt to increase your RRIF withdrawals by a fixed amount each year. Table XXVII shows how this formula works with annual 3 percent increases. Since RRIF payments usually rise each year in any event – and in doing so provide a kind of inflation protection – some financial institutions will let you take this route. But this indexed payment formula

RRIF Indexed Payments

$50,000 INVESTMENT
MALE OR FEMALE, AGE 65
DEPOSIT DATE: DECEMBER 1
FIRST MONTHLY PAYMENT: JANUARY 1
RATE OF ANNUAL INDEXING: 3%

Age	Monthly Payment	Fund Value Jan. 1	Age	Monthly Payment	Fund Value Jan. 1
66	$248.31	$50,328	84	$415.73	$52,075
67	255.76	51,246	85	422.34	51,038
68	263.43	52,145	86	429.00	49,835
69	271.34	53,019	87	435.67	48,453
70	279.48	53,865	88	442.59	46,876
71	287.86	54,676	89	449.36	45,087
72	341.00	55,447	90	456.18	43,069
73	346.67	55,615	91	463.14	40,805
74	352.46	55,725	92	469.80	38,273
75	358.34	55,772	93	476.28	35,455
76	364.69	55,749	94	482.80	32,330
77	370.50	55,644	95	481.23	28,874
78	376.66	55,459	96	419.35	25,161
79	383.05	55,181	97	365.42	21,925
80	389.55	54,801	98	318.42	19,105
81	396.01	54,310	99	277.48	16,649
82	402.29	53,698	100	241.79	14,508
83	409.11	52,959			

Total payments: $157,717.14
This stream of income assumes an 8 percent rate of interest compounded annually after each payment is withdrawn.

TABLE XXVII

is not readily available from most companies. So plan on shopping around.

If you're interested in indexed RRIFs, you should think about the level at which you will begin withdrawals. In Table XXVII, we used 3 percent. You will note that at age seventy-two the payout jumped more than 3 percent to meet the minimum requirements. From then on we had to continue with minimum withdrawals so income would last until age 100. A financial institution offering this type of fund can easily calculate a starting level that ensures your RRIF will

RRIF Fixed-Term Payout: Fifteen-Year Payout

$50,000 INVESTMENT
MALE OR FEMALE, AGE 65
DEPOSIT DATE:DECEMBER 1
FIRST MONTHLY PAYMENT: JANUARY 1
PAYOUT TERM: 15 YEARS

Age	Monthly Payment	Fund Value Jan. 1	Age	Monthly Payment	Fund Value Jan. 1
66	$469.78	$50,328	74	$469.78	$30,612
67	469.78	48,474	75	469.78	27,182
68	469.78	46,473	76	469.78	23,476
69	469.78	44,311	77	469.78	19,475
70	469.78	41,976	78	469.78	15,153
71	469.78	39,454	79	469.78	10,485
72	469.78	36,730	80	469.78	5,444
73	469.78	33,789			

Total payments: $84,561.82
This stream of income assumes 8 percent interest compounded annually after each payment is withdrawn. You can design your RRIF to reduce to a zero balance after any fixed term – five, ten, fifteen or twenty years. Withdrawals can then be structured accordingly, taking into account the rate of return on your investment.

TABLE XXVIII

last until whatever age you choose. Ask for a computer printout of the resulting payment schedule.

Payout for a fixed term

Many people considering RRIFs don't expect to live beyond age ninety. Consequently, they would like to enjoy more income early in retirement. If you feel this way – perhaps because your health is poor – you can elect to use up your RRIF through withdrawals that deplete the fund over a specified number of years.

You could, for instance, deplete your RRIF over five, ten, fifteen or twenty years, an approach that is comparable to cashing in your RRSP over a number of years, except that the fixed-term RRIF pay-out allows you to do so beyond age seventy-one. Table XXVIII il-lustrates what might happen in the case of a RRIF that will be depleted in fifteen years. This requires monthly withdrawals of

$469.78, so the fund is exhausted by age eighty. Such an approach would be perfectly sensible if you die on your eightieth birthday, but could be a disaster if you underestimate your longevity.

Consider two RRIFs

There is an alternative for many people. If you like more than one of the RRIF payment formulas we've just reviewed, consider having two RRIFs – for example, one paying on a fixed-term basis, the other providing protection beyond age eighty. After all, men on average are living until their late seventies and women until their early eighties. In looking at RRIFs, it is essential to consider your retirement income needs beyond your expected lifespan.

It is also wise to take a good look at the institutions that offer RRIFs. Not all payment formulas are offered by all companies. And remember that some institutions are not allowed by law to offer annuities. Only life insurance companies can offer life annuities, LIFs and RRIFs, while banks and trust companies can offer term-certain annuities, LIFs and RRIFs. Stockbrokers and mutual fund dealers are restricted to RRIFs and LIFs.

CHAPTER 23

RRIFs: Your Investment Choices

THERE IS MORE TO BUYING A RRIF than deciding on terms of payment. You must also wrestle with the issue of how your money is to be invested – a topic of particular interest to pensioners who want more control over their funds than they would have with an annuity. The investment alternatives under a RRIF boil down to the following:

• A daily-interest account;

• GICs;

• Mutual funds;

• A self-directed plan that includes any of the above or other investments authorized for inclusion in RRSPs and RRIFs. These include stocks, bonds, treasury bills and mortgages.

In making your RRIF investment decision, you must consider a number of factors. First and foremost is the age-old choice between risk and guarantees. Most people in their sixties, seventies and eighties should have the majority of their RRIF assets in guaranteed vehicles such as GICs, treasury bills, bonds and mortgages. Only a few can afford the short-term risks associated with the stock market. Don't rule out some exposure to growth-oriented investments over the long term. But, ask yourself what percentage of your RRIF assets you want guaranteed, and what percentage you wouldn't mind having at risk. Let's examine the investment alternatives.

Daily-interest accounts

The daily-interest account is best to be used within a RRIF only as a temporary measure when the direction of the economy is uncertain or when you are waiting to make another investment decision. Rates of return are lower than those for similar types of investments, so a daily-interest account should not be considered a long-term haven for funds.

You should be aware, however, that some financial institutions use daily-interest accounts as part of RRIFs. For example, let's say you have your RRIF invested in a five-year GIC paying 8 percent monthly. This means that each month, the interest earned on your GIC will be credited to your RRIF. If you invested $50,000, the interest earned each month under the RRIF would be $333.33. If you don't draw out all your interest, some institutions will leave the excess sitting in a daily-interest account. Therefore, the overall rate of return on your RRIF is reduced because this surplus will be earning a lower rate of interest.

Most financial institutions take a different approach. They credit you with an annual compound yield, and you then set your withdrawals at whatever level and frequency you want. All the money in the RRIF continues to earn interest at the contract rate.

Here again, it's best to obtain computer printouts to compare RRIFs. Make sure you ask whether payments flow through a daily-interest account. You don't want money sitting in such an account for too long at low interest rates.

Guaranteed investment certificates

Your RRIF can be invested in anything that qualifies for an RRSP. The most common RRIF investment is a GIC with a term of one to five years. If you choose a five-year GIC, your RRIF will be renewable every five years at prevailing interest rates. You could be investing now at between 8 and 9 percent, but find five years from now that the five-year GIC rate has dropped to 5 percent. Or risen to 12 percent. It's anyone's guess.

Taking a five-year staggered approach to RRIFs appeals to many people in their sixties and seventies. This involves initially dividing your account into five equal term deposits of one to five years and renewing each year for five years. Over the long term you will never be completely right or entirely wrong in guessing where interest rates are headed. You will average out interest rates.

The primary advantage of this approach is that part of your RRIF becomes most flexible – that is, wide open – on the renewal date. At that point, you could renew for another five years, change to another company, shift the money into an annuity or even take out cash.

Life insurance companies and a few trust companies and banks are now offering RRIFs with investment terms of longer than five years. The most common investment terms include guaranteed interest rates for ten years, fifteen years, twenty years or even for the full term of your RRIF. These plans are particularly attractive when long-term interest rates are high or poised to fall. Longer-term plans are also comforting because they free you of interest-rate worries. You could also stagger your RRIF deposits beyond one- to five-year terms (as suggested in the previous paragraph) and use a combination of short-, medium- and long-term deposits. One such approach would involve equal deposits in one-, three-, five-, ten-, and twenty-year terms to maturity.

Generally, the trade-off for a longer-term guaranteed interest rate is the cost of transferring or even cashing your plan. If you decide to transfer, sell or redeem when interest rates are higher than at the time of your original investment, check to see if you will be hit with a "market value adjustment" at the time of the change. With many institutions such a change can be made at little or no cost, with others it can be expensive.

Mutual funds

Your RRIF can invest in mutual funds, which are also called investment funds, offered by a number of financial institutions. The performance of the mutual fund will determine the yield of your RRIF, and hence have an impact on the amount you can withdraw.

If you're thinking about going this route, pick up a copy of *Understanding Mutual Funds*, part of the Financial Times Personal Finance Library, and thoroughly research the fund or funds you are considering for RRIF investments. A well-managed fund could represent a viable alternative to today's lower interest rates (relative to the 1980s). Mutual funds come in a variety of types including equity, bond, mortgage, money market and real estate.

Money market and mortgage funds are the most conservative followed by bond, balanced, and equity funds. Newer asset allocation funds, much like balanced funds, could be the answer for some of your RRIF assets. Different types of investments work best under different economic conditions. Asset allocation and balanced funds invest in a mix of investments such as stocks, bonds, mortgages and treasury bills. The fund manager makes the decisions for you. What you are trying to accomplish is to do better than a GIC in the long term while leaving it up to the professionals to decide what the asset mix should be at any point in time.

Before you jump into mutual funds for your RRIF examine management fees, administration charges, and front end and/or redemption fees. Find out who manages the fund and how long the manager has been doing so. Don't be swayed just by past performance – especially if that performance was accomplished by someone who is no longer managing the fund.

Before investing in a fund, ask yourself at what guaranteed term deposit rate would you stay with GICs? Eight percent? Ten percent? Don't use a mutual fund RRIF unless you are prepared to take a long-term approach of five to ten years. That way you will avoid the impact of short-term fluctuations in the value of your fund. Many mutual funds have averaged a 10 percent annual compound return over a ten-year period. Some life insurance company segregated funds have done equally as well and many contain minimum investment and death benefit guarantees.

Self-directed RRIFs

For those who wish to make their own investment decisions, banks, trust companies, stockbrokers and mutual fund managers offer self-directed RRIFs. Ideally, your objective would be to achieve a higher investment return with this approach than with any other. With a self-directed RRIF you can choose the investments held by your plan, making changes as the economy and your needs warrant.

Unfortunately, most people who set up self-directed RRIFs ignore them until something goes wrong. As with many self-directed RRSPs, many self-directed RRIFs have too much idle cash sitting around in low-interest investments for too long.

If you like to call your own shots and are prepared to invest in some combination of stocks, bonds, treasury bills, mutual funds and foreign securities, then a self-directed RRIF may be for you. (Remember that foreign securities cannot exceed 20 percent of the book value of your plan.)

Don't just rubber-stamp your stockbroker's suggestions. You have to be sure your plan provides your money's worth and that over the long haul you can improve on the yield you would have received on a GIC or a mutual fund.

You can move your RRIF

If you're displeased with the plan you're in, you can always move from one RRIF to another. That's not to suggest you can afford to be careless at the time the RRIF is arranged. Check out the plan for setup costs, annual administration charges and termination fees. For a list of questions to ask while RRIF shopping, see Chapter 26.

Regardless of what type of RRIF you decide on, be sure to take full advantage of its flexibility. Be sure to inquire about expenses. Will it cost you anything to increase or decrease your monthly payments? What about lump-sum withdrawals? Are they allowed? At what cost? You'll have to choose your RRIF investments carefully to be certain that extra money can be made available if required.

CHAPTER 24

The Price of Flexibility

MANY OF US ARE SO GEARED
to seeking the best return on our money that we can't see the forest
for the trees.

With RRIFs, don't jump in simply because of the interest rate. Examine the contractual conditions as well. After all, aren't you considering a RRIF because of its flexibility and the greater control it
gives you over your money? Otherwise, an annuity would suit you
just fine.

Taking out too much, too soon

People consider different payment alternatives so they can control
their money and remain flexible. However, it's not always possible
to use a RRIF to duplicate the income from an annuity.

At the time this book was written, a sixty-five-year-old buying a
joint-life annuity using $50,000 of RRSP proceeds would receive in-
come of about $402 a month, which would continue until both
husband and wife died. Usually, a guarantee of ten or fifteen years
would be attached to this annuity to provide a death benefit to the
family or estate should both die before they collect the minimum
number of payments.

Now let's say you like the idea of a guaranteed income but aren't
prepared to lock up your money in an annuity. Instead, you decide
to invest in a RRIF based on a five-year GIC earning 8.5 percent, and
you choose monthly withdrawals of $402 – the same as the joint-life
annuity would have given you. Assuming you also earn 8.5 percent
on subsequent renewals, your RRIF will run out in roughly twenty-
four years.

Most people think twenty-four years of income is good protection
for a husband and wife of sixty-five, and for most couples it is. But
what happens if either spouse is still alive at eighty-nine and needs

the income? The message is clear: carefully consider future income needs before deciding on your RRIF withdrawals.

Suppose you felt the $402 a month was not enough and you took advantage of the RRIF's flexibility to increase payments by another $100 a month. In this case, your RRIF would be used up in about fourteen years. Yes, you would have the ability to reinvest your RRIF every five years and interest rates could be up at the first renewal – but they could also be down. Taking too much out of your RRIF can shorten its lifespan dangerously.

That's why it's vital not to rush into a RRIF. Review computer projections at various monthly payments with your financial advisor to be certain that income will be there as long as you expect to need it. And whatever you do, consider the effects of living beyond normal life expectancy.

If a RRIF is still best for you, ask whether the one you have in mind is flexible enough to allow for increased payments in the future, and if it can be switched to an annuity. You have only one retirement, so ensure you have the money to finance it adequately.

How you can protect yourself

We've used the word "flexible" many times to describe RRIFs. The law allows you to increase payments or reduce them, to take out lump sums or to trade your RRIF for an annuity. Will all plans contain these provisions? What would it cost to exercise them?

We don't want to belabour the issue of the price of flexibility, but we do want to caution you about the pitfalls of RRIFs. We also want to emphasize that most people will be comfortable simply knowing that they would be able to exercise a particular provision of their RRIF contracts if necessary.

For example, you may never exercise your right under a contract to take out a lump sum or change your payment schedule. But people's needs change. Who's to say what your requirements will be ten or fifteen years from now?

Let's look at this issue in more detail, starting with a general comment: not all RRIF contracts contain the elements of flexibility allowed by law. Some of the areas of flexibility you should be concerned with are changing the payment formula, withdrawing lump sums, cashing your RRIF in full, and rolling a RRIF into an annuity.

The price of flexibility is determined by the provisions of your RRIF contract and the types of investments you choose. For ex-

ample, the most flexible types of RRIF investments are daily-interest products and those that invest in treasury bills or Canada
Savings Bonds. With such plans, cash is available on short notice.
But holding the short-term RRIF assets that give you the most flexibility means you may use up your money much sooner than age
ninety if, for example, the long-term interest-rate direction is
downward.

How do you avoid this problem? By having a mix of assets under
one RRIF or in a number of RRIFs. For example, you may want to
invest in a series of one-year to five-year GICs with staggered maturity dates. If you go this route, investment decisions must be made
every year, but you have the option to take out large amounts of
money on maturity dates if the need arises.

Five-year GICS, as well as interest-rate guarantees offered by life
insurance companies for ten or fifteen years, are generally 2 percent
to 4 percent higher than short-term rates.

With these longer-term investments you don't have the degree of
flexibility of short-term vehicles, but you do get flexibility at renewal. For example, with a five-year GIC you can renew for a different term, change to another company, withdraw cash or turn your
RRIF into an annuity. Some companies levy termination fees of $25
to $100, but most give you the freedom to do as you wish without
charge.

Keep in mind that trying to make changes in GIC-type plans
before the renewal date may be difficult or impossible. Some companies, especially trust firms, will not allow you out of your RRIF
investment until renewal. Others levy a market value adjustment or
expense adjustment. Life insurance companies will generally grant
you more flexibility as most of their RRIFs are redeemable.

A market value adjustment is a modification of the value of your
RRIF that occurs when a gap opens between the interest rate of your
original investment and the rate currently offered by the company
holding your RRIF. At the time you arrange a RRIF, your financial
institution makes an investment to match its obligation to provide
you with a guaranteed investment rate for the term you chose. If
you change your mind and want out, the company must do one of
two things to come up with the money: it must sell the investment
underlying your RRIF at its current market value or use money that
could be invested at the current higher interest rates. In either case,
the company will face a loss that it passes along to you.

In its booklet, *Retirement: As You'd Like It,* the Canadian Life and Health Insurance Association provides an excellent example of the effect of a market value adjustment. (For information on obtaining CLHIA publications, see the appendix, Where to Get More Information.) In the association's example, a $50,000 twenty-year government bond yielding 10 percent is purchased at par. At maturity the buyer will get the $50,000 back, but he also receives $2,500 in interest each six months.

What happens if the investor wants to sell the bond five years after purchase, when interest rates are 12 percent? Since the market value of the bond has dropped to compensate for the low 10 percent yield, anyone buying the bond from the original purchaser would pay only $44,600 – a discount of $5,400. A new buyer would earn the prevailing 12 percent interest rate for the remaining fifteen years to maturity through a combination of the $5,400 discount and the 10 percent interest the bond pays. In the CLHIA example, the $5,400 drop in the bond's value is the market value adjustment.

But what if interest rates have fallen since the original purchase? You may win in some cases, but not in all.

Let's follow through on the CLHIA's example. If the twenty-year bond is sold five years after purchase, when interest rates have fallen to 8 percent, the bond would be worth $56,800, or $6,800 more than the original investment. Unfortunately, not all companies will pass along all of this gain to the RRIF owner.

Companies take different approaches to market value adjustments (also known as asset depreciation charges or interest adjustments).

The factors that enter into their calculations are the difference in interest rates between the purchase date and the time you want out, and the length of time until the investment matures. Our survey of major life insurers shows that three companies – Canada Life, Mutual Life and Great-West Life – pass along investment gains to the RRIF owner. Others vary in their practices.

Some even impose an expense charge that wipes out the increase in value. This means you may be better off waiting until renewal time before converting to an annuity or making unscheduled withdrawals.

Be wary of taxes

While some people will eventually convert their RRIFs into annuities, others may want to withdraw lump sums. We don't recommend that you view your RRIF as being as flexible as a bank account because even a partial withdrawal will be fully taxable.

In the case of fixed-term investments, you face additional costs to get at your funds.

You can take comfort from the fact that partial RRIF withdrawals are possible but for flexibility, it may be best to hold assets such as Canada Savings Bonds outside your RRIF and use these if you need money. You'll pay tax on the interest but will not face an expense charge or market value adjustment.

When it comes to changing the payment stream provided by your RRIF, trust companies, banks and life insurance companies vary widely in their practices. Some let you modify payments before a GIC matures, while others won't. Of those that allow changes, many levy fees or market value adjustments. As a result, it is better to accurately estimate your income requirements and set your payments accordingly.

Some companies may be quite flexible on income requirements, but rigid on early withdrawals. With many financial institutions, you can change the pay-out option of your RRIF at any time without cost. On the other hand, most RRIF contracts penalize you or simply don't allow it if you decide to get out before the end of an investment term.

When it comes to mutual funds and self-directed RRIFs, the price of flexibility depends on the type of investment.

Shares of a mutual fund can usually be sold quickly at their current market value. Payment formulas are also quite flexible, although not all fund managers offer all payment options. Beware of the "back-end load", a fee for getting out that is levied by some funds. Many funds solve this potential problem by allowing up to 10 percent of your RRIF balance to be withdrawn annually, free of redemption fees.

Self-directed RRIFs can also be quite flexible. Stocks and bonds in a self-directed RRIF can be sold to provide cash. Both are sold at current market value, which could be substantially lower or higher than at the time of the original investment. The difficulty, however, is that market conditions may not be right at the time a withdrawal is scheduled. This often necessitates keeping sufficient money liquid in, perhaps a low-interest bearing treasury bill, to meet you scheduled withdrawals.

If you're thinking of buying an annuity with your RRIF proceeds, you should know that in the year of roll-over you must withdraw at least the minimum from your RRIF to comply with government regulations. Under current rules, if you're seventy-five and have $100,000 in a RRIF, you must take out 7.85 percent of the value of the plan during that year to comply with the minimum payout requirements. This would come to $7,850; no more than $92,150 could be transferred tax-free to an annuity.

CHAPTER 25

Turning Spousal RRSPs into RRIFs

WHEN IT COMES TO TURNING a spousal RRSP into a RRIF, you may have to give up some flexibility. And you could walk into a trap if you are not wary.

First, let's take a look at spousal RRSPs. Making contributions to a spousal RRSP works especially well when one spouse has a pension plan and the other doesn't. Instead of making RRSP contributions to his or her own RRSP, the person who belongs to a pension plan puts all or some of that contribution into a spousal plan. This counts as part of the contributor's annual RRSP limit and is deductible for income tax purposes in the usual way.

The concept behind a spousal RRSP is to end up at retirement with taxable income that is attributable to both spouses. This way, the tax bill is often lower than in cases where all income is taxed in the hands of one spouse. For example, a family will have more after-tax income to enjoy in retirement if the husband and wife each have $15,000 of income, rather than one spouse having the entire $30,000. The marginal tax rate is lower on each of the $15,000 portions, and splitting income allows both spouses to claim the pension credit. But the Income Tax Act, in a measure intended to keep the spousal RRSP from being used as a way to reduce tax during a person's working years, stipulates that if a spousal RRSP is cashed within three years from the time of the original contributions, proceeds are taxable in the contributor's hands.

This might work well for its intended purpose, but the three-year requirement can create problems in winding down a spousal RRSP at retirement time. In choosing a RRIF under these circumstances, you must be aware that some of the RRIF income could be taxed back to you if you were the contributor. If you contributed to your spouse's RRSP in the current year or in the two previous years and the plan is converted to a RRIF, your spouse should withdraw only the minimum for the first three years.

This way, the family enjoys the benefits of splitting income between spouses. If your spouse takes more than the minimum, you will normally be required to include in your income (and be taxed on it) the excess of payments over the minimum RRIF income up to your spousal contribution in the current and two previous years.

This requirement does not apply if the money is received because of death or marriage breakdown.

Let's take an example. Assume you made spousal RRSP contributions totalling $4,000 for the current and two preceding years, and the minimum required to be withdrawn from your spouse's RRIF in the first year is $2,500. Instead of the minimum, your spouse takes out $6,000. The excess of $3,500 is taxable in your hands. One other critical point: since there is no minimum withdrawal required by law in the year in which a RRIF is entered into, any amount taken out by your spouse during that year could be taxed back to you, the contributor. Once you know about this pitfall, it's easy to avoid.

Consider starting your minimum RRIF withdrawals in the calendar year following the year your spouse opens the plan. Alternatively, use a non-cashable annuity instead of a RRIF and no attribution will occur. If your spouse has another RRIF bought with personal RRSP funds, all the better. In this case, more than the minimum can be withdrawn from this RRIF without increasing your tax bill.

CHAPTER 26

A RRIF Checklist: What to Look For

DO NOT RUSH INTO A RRIF. Sit down with a qualified advisor who will take the time to provide helpful, informative advice. The following checklist will give you an idea of some of the points that should be covered.

1. Payment choices. How is minimum income determined with a RRIF? What payment alternatives are available, such as interest-only, smoothing-factor or fixed-term payments? How often can you receive cheques?

2. Investment alternatives. What types of investments are allowed under the RRIF you have in mind? What return, in percentage terms, can you expect on your money? How does a term-deposit-type RRIF work? Can you get an interest-rate guarantee for more than five years? Should I consider a self-directed RRIF? Are mutual funds a suitable investment?

3. Protecting your spouse. If you're married, does the plan provide for payments to continue to your spouse after your death? Is a lump sum payable to your spouse instead? Would your spouse have ownership rights after your death? (Certain RRIFs may not allow a surviving spouse to make changes before renewal.)

4. Fees and charges. Are there fees to set up the RRIF? Annual administration fees? Fees for lump-sum withdrawals? A fee for issuing cheques? What are the charges for cancelling your RRIF or taking out a lump sum? How about charges for changing the payment period from, say, monthly to semi-annually?

5. Flexibility. Does the contract allow you to change the amount of payments? Can you collapse the RRIF to change companies or buy an annuity? If it's a term-deposit RRIF you're considering, is the plan flexible before maturity – can you, for instance, change the payment schedule or switch to an annuity? Are you allowed to withdraw lump sums? If you want to change the type of RRIF investment, do you have a full range of choices? What are they?

6. Death benefit. Is the lump-sum benefit to your spouse or other heirs guaranteed? Is there a charge for cancelling the RRIF after your death? How long after your death would it take to settle a claim? What documentation would your family or estate need? What amount will be taxable in your estate?

7. Transfer value. How is the value of your RRIF determined if you decide to transfer it to another company or buy an annuity?

8. Safety. How secure is your money? Does insurance provided by the Canada Deposit Insurance Corp. or CompCorp apply to the money in your RRIF? Is there an advantage to dealing with a life insurance company? If so, what is it?

9. Service. Can the salesperson give you an illustration of what the payments would be? Would you receive a certificate or policy? If you decide to make changes once RRIF payments begin, whom do you contact? Would you get regular statements on the status of your RRIF? If it's a term-deposit RRIF, how much notice would you get before renewal time? Can the payments be deposited directly to your bank account instead of paid by cheques, which can be delayed in the mail?

10. Your advisor. What are the qualifications of the person who wants to sell you a RRIF? Does he or she specialize in retirement income services, or offer other products and services as well? How long has the person been in business? Can references be provided? How is the person paid? Who would help your spouse (or family or estate) at the time of your death?

CHAPTER 27

RRIFs and Your Estate

IN AN EARLIER CHAPTER, WE discussed estate values for a person who dies while owning an annuity purchased with RRSP funds. In this chapter, we'll examine the payment of RRIF proceeds upon death.

Let's assume you are married and you name your spouse as successor annuitant – in other words the successor payee – under the RRIF contract. When you die, payments continue to your spouse until the end of the original RRIF term. The payments are taxable in your spouse's hands for the years in which they are received.

However, if your spouse is not named as the successor annuitant but is the beneficiary of your RRIF, he or she can use the death benefit proceeds to buy another RRIF, a life annuity (with or without a guarantee period) or a term-certain annuity to age ninety. If your spouse has not reached age seventy-one at the time of your death, the proceeds of your RRIF can be transferred to an RRSP instead. In any event, everything can be rolled over tax-free to your surviving spouse (a term that, as we've mentioned earlier, can include a common-law spouse with whom you have lived for at least a year).

The significance of designating your spouse as successor annuitant is that payments will continue automatically. This avoids any disruption in the process and does not negate the terms of the original investment. Since a person can now have more than one RRIF, this can be done even if your spouse already has a RRIF.

It's a different story if you're single, widowed or divorced, or if the beneficiary is one of your children or grandchildren. If the beneficiary of your RRIF is one of your children or grandchildren who is considered a dependant, the full amount can be transferred as a lump sum to the child. The child has the option to spread the tax by purchasing a special annuity paying out equal annual

The RRIF Maximizer

MALE, AGE 71 (NON-SMOKER)
FEMALE, AGE 70 (SMOKER)
RRIF INVESTMENT: $300,000
MARGINAL TAX RATE: 40%
RRIF YIELD: 8.20%
PAYOUT: INTEREST ONLY

Age	Without Maximizer Monthly Income	Without Maximizer Estate Value	With Maximizer Monthly Income	With Maximizer Estate Value
71	$1,230	$180,000	$1,037	$300,000
75	1,230	180,000	1,037	300,000
80	1,270	177,194	1,077	297,494
85	1,418	163,800	1,225	283,800
90	1,522	136,465	1,329	256,465

The "maximizer" is a life insurance policy insuring both husband and wife and providing for a tax-free death benefit to family or estate following the death of both spouses. In this example, the monthly premium based on coverage of $120,000 is $193. This "joint second-death" policy is available from a number of companies. The rates quoted here are those of Transamerica Life.

TABLE XXIX

instalments until age eighteen. No limit applies if the child is dependent by reason of physical or mental handicap.

A dependent handicapped child can then roll the proceeds tax-free into an RRSP or buy an annuity or RRIF. Any proceeds not rolled into one of these tax-deferral vehicles are taxable in the hands of the child for the year received. Any remaining proceeds from your RRIF not transferred in this way will be taxable to your estate.

Taxman gets his bite

In any other situation where your RRIF beneficiary is not your spouse or a dependent child or grandchild, the full value of your RRIF will be taxable to your estate. This means that whatever is left in your RRIF is added to your income in the year of death and taxed as if you had earned it that year.

You can see that the taxman certainly gets his bite, especially if you stay with the minimum-payment formula or some other conservative payment schedule. Therefore, you should ask yourself whether it makes sense to take less income now and leave more for Revenue Canada.

Let's take the example of a seventy-one-year-old married man who uses a $300,000 RRSP to buy a RRIF. He decides to draw only the interest from his RRIF, which earns 8.2 percent. This person is in a 40 percent tax bracket, so on each monthly withdrawal of $2,050 ($24,600 a year interest on $300,000), he loses $820 in income tax. This means his net monthly income from his RRIF, on an interest-only basis, is $1,230.

As we illustrated in an earlier chapter, on an interest-only basis you can continue withdrawals at the same rate each year until age seventy-seven. After that, payments must increase. If this man and his wife both die during their seventies, the $300,000 RRIF (the original amount is still intact because he has been withdrawing interest only) would be taxed in the hands of the estate at 40 percent – generating $120,000 in taxes. As a result, the estate would be left with $180,000.

You may think that a $180,000 estate is sufficient, but if this couple's objective is to leave an estate as large as possible, is the RRIF the best means? Yes it is, but look at Table XXIX.

The monthly income and the estate value after tax are shown in the first two columns. But if husband and wife are both insurable, an interesting new twist is available. For a monthly premium of about $193, they can buy $120,000 of life insurance that will pay a tax-free death benefit to their estate after both have died.

This $120,000, plus what's left in the RRIF after tax, equals the $300,000 they started with. This type of life insurance is known as "joint second-death coverage". For the purposes of the table, we have used rates from Transamerica Life, a leading issuer of this type of coverage. But many other companies offer similar policies, so shop around.

This concept has been tagged "the RRIF maximizer," and it's not for everyone. Obviously, you have to be in reasonable health, and premiums vary depending on whether you smoke. But it's worthy of consideration if leaving an estate is your major goal. The "maximizer" gives you flexibility in payments from your RRIF by allowing you to draw interest only, while providing the maximum amount to your estate.

You might think that because you can now extend the RRIF pay-out for life that the life insurance is no longer necessary. This is not the case since what you are insuring is the tax liability at death, which will still exist. If, in our example, interest only was used with an age-100 payout, roughly one-quarter of the original investment would still be available for the estate at age 100. Since this is taxable, life insurance would restore the capital used.

Whether you're interested in the RRIF maximizer or not, don't be fooled into thinking that your estate will get everything after you and your spouse die. If you're single, widowed or divorced, the tax-man usually becomes your unnamed beneficiary. With no spouse to roll your funds over to, the full amount of your plans must be included in the final tax return and taxes paid before your beneficiaries receive their share.

CHAPTER 28

Turning Over a New LIF – Life Income Funds

MANY CANADIANS HAVE locked-in RRSPs, or locked-in retirement accounts (LIRA) as they are called in some provinces, as a result of removing their pension plan dollars from a pension plan when they leave an employer. There is little difference between these two vehicles other than the degree of control the various provinces exert over them. (Ontario, British Columbia, Nova Scotia and Newfoundland use the term locked-in RRSP.) You cannot simply take your pension benefit entitlement as cash, both federal and provincial pension legislation contain restrictions that ensure you will not, in the government's view, squander away your future security. Instead you must move the money into a special RRSP account which contains restrictions similar to those in a pension plan. Most significantly, they are "locked-in." You are not able to cash-out your plan before retirement as you can a regular RRSP.

The pension legislation which governs your locked-in funds will be that of the province where you worked and earned benefits. A person who spent his career in Ontario and retired to beautiful British Columbia would be subject to Ontario rules. Prince Edward Island does not have any pension legislation so pension options are governed by the individual employer plans and the federal pension rules. Those who work in the Yukon or the Northwest Territories or in industries subject to federal regulation, such as airlines, banks and railways, are subject to the Pension Benefits Standards Act referred to in chapter eight.

Until recently your only retirement income option with a locked-in RRSP was to purchase a lifetime annuity – a requirement that did not appeal to Canadians who wanted to control their money. Now you can have a life income fund, the LIF. The LIF was first introduced in Quebec in 1991 and has since been implemented in Alberta, British Columbia, New Brunswick, Ontario, Manitoba,

Life Income Fund

$50,000 INVESTMENT
MALE OR FEMALE: AGE 65
DEPOSIT DATE: DECEMBER 1
FIRST MONTHLY PAYMENT: JANUARY 1

Age	Fund at Beginning of the Year	Yearly Income	Minimum Income a Year	Maximum Income a Year (8.12%)
65	$50,000.00	$ 0.00	$ 0.00	$ 353.74
66	50,288.14	2,011.56	2,011.56	4,314.96
67	51,721.27	2,155.08	2.155.08	4,489.92
68	53,105.81	2,308.92	2,308.92	4,669.20
69	54,427.66	2,473.92	2,473.92	4,852.68
70	55,670.85	2,651.04	2,651.04	5,040.12
71	56,817.29	2,840.88	2,840.88	5,231.28
72	57,847.02	4,269.12	4,269.12	5,425.56
73	57,466.99	4,298.52	4,298.52	5,501.16
74	57,029.86	4,328.52	4,328.52	5,583.84
75	56,531.00	4,358.52	4,358.52	5,674.92
76	55,966.10	4,393.32	4,393.32	5,776.08
77	55,325.55	4,420.56	4,420.56	5,889.00
78	54,611.90	4,450.92	4,450.92	6,016.92
79	53,816.79	4,482.96	4,482.96	6,162.96
80	52,932.79	4,515.12	4,515.12	6,331.56

TABLE XXX

Saskatchewan and Nova Scotia. Not only can you establish a LIF with a locked-in RRSP or LIRA, you can purchase a LIF with your pension funds if your plan has been amended to permit the purchase of a LIF. If you're interested in this option speak to the benefits coordinator in your human resources department.

The life income fund is essentially a RRIF with some limitations. First, you must be at least fifty-five years of age to set up a LIF, whereas there isn't a minimum age requirement with a RRIF. Second, you must withdraw at least a minimum amount each year commencing no later than the end of the calendar year following the establishment of the plan, as with a RRIF. However, unlike the RRIF, under the LIF there is a maximum income that can be paid out in any one year. This maximum is determined by a formula which applies a term-certain-to-age-ninety annuity factor to the fund value at the beginning of each year. In other words, the maximum income which you can receive each year is the amount you would receive if you purchase an annuity-to-age-ninety.

This limitation on the maximum withdrawal means that you cannot cash-out a LIF as you can a RRIF; more important, it ensures that there is still money in the LIF when you reach age eighty, the point at which you must convert your LIF to an annuity in most provinces. Consistent with pension legislation, the annuity must be a joint-and-last-survivor annuity if you are married. This ensures protection for your spouse. In Ontario, the annuity must allow for at least 60 percent of the monthly income to continue to your spouse, unless the spouse chooses to waive this right. Your spouse must also be named beneficiary so that his or her benefits are protected even if you die before converting your LIF to an annuity.

Alberta and Saskatchewan also offer a LRIF, the life retirement income fund. The LRIF is similar to the LIF but does not require the purchase of a lifetime annuity at age eighty. Rather, you can continue to receive the stipulated LIF-type payments until death, an option that will please people who do not wish to buy an annuity.

Table XXX illustrates the payout under a LIF assuming an investment return of 7 percent compounded annually. In this example our sixty-five year old withdraws the minimum amount until age eighty, at which point the $50,000 originally invested has increased to $52,933. It is a small increase but it demonstrates that you can maintain your capital until you are forced to convert to an annuity. At any particular point in time the LIF planholder can increase withdrawals up to the maximum shown but the fund value would begin to decline. If the maximum withdrawal was taken every year only 85 percent of the original $50,000 would be available at age eighty for conversion to an annuity.

You will note under the column "Maximum Income Per Annum" that 8.12 percent appears. This is not the investment return, it is the annuity-to-age-ninety factor which is used to determine the maximum amount you can withdraw from your LIF in a particular year, as we mentioned earlier. This factor, known as the CANSIM rate, is compiled by Statistics Canada and published monthly in the Bank of Canada Review. It represents the average rates obtained on long-term bonds issued by the Government of Canada for the preceding month.

The appeal of the LIF lies in your ability to invest the funds as you choose. Your investment choices are the same as for RRIFs, ranging from guaranteed term deposits to mutual funds. As you make your investment decisions, bear in mind that your investment time frame is to age eighty. And, since you can purchase your annuity before you reach age eighty, you should keep an eye on interest rates. You'll want to buy your LIF when rates are high – and avoid being forced to cash-out when rates are low.

The popularity of the LIF will surely increase dramatically over the next decade. The ability to control the investment of your money coupled with greater flexibility will appeal to Canadians who do not wish to be forced into an annuity.

CHAPTER 29

Comparing RRIFs With Annuities

NOW THAT YOU UNDERSTAND the basic options available when you are converting your RRSPs to monthly retirement cheques, it's time to decide which of these options are best for you. Let's summarize the advantages and drawbacks of annuities and RRIFs, then look at some of the things you should consider before making your decision.

Annuity advantages

• Payments can be guaranteed for your lifetime, until both you and your spouse have died or to age ninety.
• No management is required.
• You don't have to worry about the ups and downs of the stock market or interest rates.

Annuity drawbacks

• Annuities require you to give up control of your capital, although cashable annuities are now available.
• They're generally less flexible than RRIFs.
• They usually have a lower estate value than RRIFs.

RRIF advantages

• RRIFs allow you to design your own pension.
• You can vary payments.
• You can change companies.
• You control the types of investments.
• RRIFs generally produce a larger estate value, depending on the payment schedule and the options you choose.

RRIF drawbacks
• A RRIF may require ongoing management, depending on the investment type and your changing circumstances.
• Taking too much money out of a RRIF too soon may result in your outliving it.

Your choice: RRIFs and/or an annuity
Consider your annuity and/or RRIF purchase with the utmost care. A wrong decision could affect you throughout your life, hurt your spouse following your death and reduce the value of both your estates. Some purchase options should not even be considered in certain circumstances.

Products and interest rates tend to preoccupy buyers of retirement options. You'd be better off considering which alternatives best meet your needs. We have found that people who are about to wind down their RRSPs are concerned about:
• The income they will receive immediately.
• Financial security in the future and whether income will be adequate if inflation takes off.
• What will be left after death.

To make the proper decision, you need to think about your future income needs. It's a task that can be almost as tedious as drawing up a personal budget. The best place to start is to list all the sources of income you anticipate for the rest of your life. Include CPP and OAS benefits when they kick in (including federal and provincial supplements), and take into account any years of reduced income.

How will inflation affect your sources of income? Your government pensions will be fully indexed – or at least they have been so far – and you might even have an employer pension with limited indexing. But remember: if you have a $20,000 annual pension today, you may need $30,000 a year a decade from now simply to stay even in terms of buying power. See Table I in Chapter 2 for an idea of how inflation will affect your income needs.

To help combat the effects of inflation, you must keep some of your retirement funds in a plan that will provide automatic income increases or give you the flexibility to index your own pension as you see fit.

This might call for an indexed annuity. With this type, monthly income increases each year at a 4 percent guaranteed rate, or according to a formula tied to inflation. Alternatively, you can use a

RRIF to set your own indexing, since you can take out whatever amount is necessary.

The next issue to consider in choosing annuities and RRIFs is your age. If you're married, your spouse's age is also important. Ask yourself: "How long am I going to require income?" You can't afford to assume you'll need income for ten years, go through your capital accordingly, and discover that you're still around when your money runs out.

If you're in your early sixties, you could have a third of your life ahead of you. This factor alone makes careful planning vital. If you are older, consider the average life expectancies shown in Chart I in chapter 2.

Some annuity and RRIF options are terrible choices for people in poor health. For example, you wouldn't want to arrange a life annuity with no guarantee if you are in poor health and your spouse will require income after your death. But if your spouse is in poor health, it may be acceptable to take a slightly riskier option on the assumption that he or she will die before you. Still, you shouldn't play the odds; you could easily be wrong. Build in guarantees.

The question which you might ask now that we have legislation on the horizon for lifetime RRIFs is: Are annuities still a viable alternative? Yes, for a number of reasons. RRIFs provide flexibility in terms of how much to withdraw along with control of your money, an important "plus", albeit at times only a psychological one. But RRIFs also require a decision on how to invest your money – a decision which not everyone is capable of now, and which most of us will be less capable of as we age.

Even if you are not ready for an annuity now, do not rule it out altogether. RRIFs can be converted to annuities – the benefit of a lifetime income with no management required may be more appealing in your later years.

Secondly, the value of the minimum payout RRIF may start to deplete as early as age seventy-five at an 8 percent yield. Further, even though the government has effectively handed us a "lifetime" RRIF, the income from that RRIF will decline quickly beyond age ninety-four. With an increasing percentage of the population living beyond age ninety, there will be a need for the guaranteed income that only an annuity can provide.

Finally, annuities provide higher incomes than RRIFs when your RRIF withdrawals are anywhere between the minimum and the interest earned in the plan. This is because annuities are based on yields from long-term instruments of ten to twenty years. At the same time they generally provide a smaller estate than RRIFs. The challenge with the RRIF however, lies in the tradeoff between income today and leaving an estate.

Trying to duplicate the income from an annuity in your RRIF may mean that your RRIF does not last as long as you want it to.

In these circumstances you might be better to purchase an annuity and look at alternative means of maximizing the benefit to your family or estate, if that is important to you.

The issue boils down to whether the higher amount of the payments from an annuity and the guarantees therein are attractive enough to you to make up for the loss of flexibility and control you would achieve through a RRIF. Keep an open mind about annuities. Usually the concern is loss of capital. But consider what your bank does when it loans you money in a mortgage. Over twenty-five years it receives a stream of monthly payments with nothing left at the end. Does the bank view this transaction as losing its capital or does it consider it a poor investment? Not at all. On the other hand, if you as a sixty-five year old purchase a term certain annuity to age ninety – a twenty-five year payout – the result is the same as with mortgage. Capital is returned as part of the stream of payments. Nothing is "lost". Trading off some of that stream in return for a guaranteed income for life may be attractive to some people.

Since annuities and RRIFs have their pros and cons, your personal needs should dictate which route to take. A combination of the two may suit your requirements.

Investing in retirement

When it comes to investing, it's also a good idea not to gamble. For most retired people, a mix of at least 70 to 80 percent guaranteed investments and 20 to 30 percent growth investments is best. After all, this is your retirement income. If you lose it, you're not likely to have the time or resources to recover financially.

If you don't have previous stock-investing experience, now isn't the time to start playing the market. On the other hand, if you have a proven track record in mutual funds or managing your self-directed RRSP, you can easily continue this approach in a self-directed RRIF. Just remember to pay particular attention to what portion of retirement income is to be at risk and what part should be guaranteed.

Whether you have investments outside your RRSPs has an obvious impact on how much you will want to take out of your RRSPs through annuities and/or RRIFs. Be aware, however, that in most circumstances it will be best to first use your non-tax-sheltered assets (the investments held outside an RRSP) and use your RRSP funds later. Because your RRSP is sheltered from tax, it makes sense to leave it intact for as long as possible.

If you're living on your cash investments and continuing to build up your RRSP, you must always have an emergency fund. This could consist of investments such as Canada Savings Bonds and treasury bills, which are readily converted to cash. The amount will vary according to your circumstances and your cash comfort level.

Look at your life insurance

Many people in their sixties and seventies want to go into hiding when they hear the words "life insurance." They realize that the old-style life policies they bought were a poor investment, and they think they're too old to get the more attractive modern policies now offered at reasonable premiums.

A competent financial advisor can help you review your life policies and recommend a course of action. Life insurance remains one of the best sources of immediate cash for a widow or an estate. It can be used to pay income tax, legal and accounting fees, probate fees, and pay off any debt.

If you need liquidity in your estate, keep your insurance policies; if not, consider freeing up some of the cash value and putting it to better use at current interest rates.

Protecting your spouse

A person winding down an RRSP often asks whether a joint-life annuity should be chosen to protect a spouse, or whether an "insured annuity" should be chosen instead.

The joint-life annuity provides income for as long as you or your spouse are alive, and can have minimum guarantees built in to provide estate values in case both of you die prematurely. The insured annuity is one in which you choose a life annuity with no guarantees; that is, your monthly income stops on the day you die.

At the same time you buy an insurance policy that provides tax-free proceeds to your spouse or estate upon your death, which is when the life annuity stops.

Someone considering the concept may hope to turn potentially taxable dollars (the commuted value of an annuity or RRIF at the time of death) into tax-free insurance proceeds for family or estate. This makes sense if he qualifies medically for reasonably priced life insurance before selecting this option.

Keep in mind, however, that an insured annuity puts more commission into your insurance agent's pocket. Be sure the arrangement makes sense from your perspective. To compare the joint-life annuity with the insured annuity alternative, refer to Table XIII in chapter 15.

CHAPTER 30

How Safe Is Your Money?

RETIREES DO TEND TO WORRY
about the safety of their money. So they should. A loss of retirement funds can be devastating at an age when you have little time and few resources to recover from financial disaster.

This concern has intensified in recent years because of widespread publicity about troubled North American financial institutions, such as the two Alberta banks that collapsed in 1985, and the 1991 collapse of Standard Trust Co., and the more recent problems surrounding Central Guaranty Trust and Royal Trust.

It makes sense, then, that when you arrange an annuity or RRIF you should be comfortable with the degree of protection your investments will have. This may mean settling for a competitive return from a reliable institution, rather than making financial decisions based solely on the rate of return available from investments.

The 1986 changes opening up the flexibility of RRIFs and annuities, in combination with the deregulation of financial services over the past few years, have encouraged institutions that previously ignored RRIFs and annuities to enter the market with a variety of products. In terms of safety, all of these institutions are not equal. Let's take a look.

Insurance companies

Only insurance companies can offer life annuities. They also offer RRIFs and term-certain annuities. In the past, these companies were bastions of financial security. You had less cause for concern over the safety of your retirement nest egg with a life insurance company than with a bank, trust company or any other financial institution. That's because life insurers operate in a way that makes them less prone to disaster. Recently however, we have seen the windup of three life insurance companies, The Coopérants in Quebec, Sovereign Life in Alberta, and Confederation Life in Ontario as well as concerns over the well-being of other companies.

If you hand over your RRSP funds to buy an annuity, the insurance company is required to meet strict solvency regulations. It must establish a reserve for every dollar owed to you. Furthermore, life insurance companies invest heavily in approved securities meeting exacting quality standards, such as federal government long-term bonds. Not only are these bonds the ultimate in security, they provide the long-term investments needed to match the needs of the annuity buyer who chooses a term guaranteed for life.

Just the same, in 1990 the life insurance industry introduced a consumer protection plan to protect policyholders, within limits, against the loss of benefits should a member company ever become insolvent and go out of business. In effect, it's insurance for your insurance. Through a federally incorporated private company called Canadian Life and Health Insurance Compensation Corp., dubbed CompCorp, the plan will provide:

• Insurance on a life insurance policy of up to $200,000.

• A lump sum of up to $60,000 for someone who chooses to cash in a RRSP, RRIF or non-registered life insurance policy, including life insurance cash values.

• A one-time-only option to owners of RRIFs and cashable annuities to forego the $60,000 cash withdrawal referred to above in exchange for a life annuity insured for up to $2,000 a month if the member insurer becomes insolvent.

• Up to $2,000 a month for someone already receiving income from a non-cashable life annuity or disability income policy.

• Up to $60,000 in total payments for health benefits other than disability income.

CompCorp has some unique features. For example, the limits apply to each person separately. The example given in CompCorp's useful booklet refers to a joint-life annuity where a couple are receiving "an annuity of $5,000 a month while both are alive, reducing to $3,000 a month after one dies."

In this example, the protection would be $4,000 a month while both are alive and $2,000 afterwards. Secondly, RRSPs, RRIFs, and pension policies are combined for the purpose of the $60,000 protection described above. Spousal RRSPs would fall under the limit that applies to the spouse, not the contributor.

One last point: policies issued before CompCorp was founded are protected. More information on this consumer protection plan can be obtained by writing to CompCorp at 20 Queen Street West, Suite 2500, Toronto, Ontario M5H 3R3.

Banks and trust companies

Banks and trust companies can offer only one type of annuity – the term-certain-to-ninety. Only a few offer these annuities, and the reserve requirements for these institutions are not the same as for insurance companies. They do, however, have to maintain a conservative ratio of assets to liabilities.

The Canada Deposit Insurance Corp. provides coverage on most bank and trust company deposits with terms of five years or less, but this insurance doesn't apply to term-certain annuities.

How safe is a RRIF?

The safety of your RRIF depends on the assets in which it is invested. Let's look at the investment alternatives.

Life insurance company RRIFs: These RRIFs fall under the solvency requirements discussed earlier in this chapter for annuities and the consumer protection plan limit of $60,000. However, RRIFs tied to life insurance company investment funds – called segregated funds, but similar to mutual funds – don't carry blanket guarantees. Some have minimum death benefit and maturity value guarantees in case your investment doesn't pan out. As with mutual funds, you must look at the track record of the fund and its manager.

Bank, trust company and credit union RRIFs: On guaranteed investment certificates with terms of up to five years, Canada Deposit Insurance Corp. coverage applies (or similar provincial coverage in the case of credit unions) at member institutions, with a limit of $60,000.

Some institutions will structure your RRIF so that you have $120,000 of insurance by placing half your money with an affiliated company. If they don't, it's a good idea to put some money in another company so it's all insured.

Don't forget: the original contribution, plus any interest earned, should be less than the $60,000 limit. If your RRIF is approaching this size, consider shifting some money elsewhere.

If your RRIF is in a mutual fund at a bank, trust company or credit union, you have no deposit insurance and are relying on the strength of the assets in the investment and the manager's savvy.

Self-directed RRIFs: The key to safety here is the underlying assets, such as stocks, bonds, mutual funds, Canada Savings Bonds or treasury bills. With Canada Savings Bonds and federal treasury bills, for example, the federal government is guaranteeing the investment – and that's about the best guarantee you can have. With stocks and mutual funds, you're relying on the performance of particular companies and funds.

Mutual fund RRIFs: In the case of a RRIF-eligible mutual fund (as opposed to having a mutual fund in a self-directed RRIF), the performance of the assets again determines the result.

While there are no guarantees, the diversification and professional management you get with mutual funds may leave you in a better financial position over the long run than GICs. Keep in mind, however, that you must be able to weather short-term ups and downs in a fund's value.

CHAPTER 31

Shopping for the Best Rates

THERE IS A CONFUSING ARRAY of annuities, LIFs and RRIFs available. Shopping for the best rates can be frustrating. There are more than 160 life insurance companies in Canada, although at any given time only twenty or so are offering competitive annuities. Others will be marketing annuities with incomes that are far from the best and the remainder will not be quoting rates.

All types of annuities are offered by life insurance companies. Trust companies and banks sell only fixed-term annuities to age ninety.

Request a survey

How do you know if the product you are looking at is competitive? Ask for a survey of at least ten companies, similar to Table IX in Chapter 15. These independent, computerized quotations are readily available to annuity brokers and insurance agents. CANNEX Financial Exchanges Ltd., which supplied data for the annuity and RRIF tables in this book, sells quotations to brokers and agents.

A survey typically lists twenty competitive companies for an annuity or RRIF option in which a customer is interested. A survey can also show the monthly income from all options offered by one company. However, your broker or agent must still contact some companies individually because they don't participate in computerized surveys.

At the time of writing, it was necessary to get telephone quotations from the following: Prudential Life of England, Zurich Life, and AEterna Life. In addition, a few companies – including London Life and Prudential of England – sell only through their own agents. A good annuity broker can make arrangements with agents of these companies.

Consider only the monthly income when you shop for an annuity. One company promising 9 percent may have higher expenses and different actuarial assumptions, resulting in a lower monthly income than that received from a company offering 8.5 percent.

Ask your broker what insurance company sponsors his or her license to do business. (If you're dealing with a company agent, the answer will be obvious.) Sponsoring companies pay commissions and bonuses to their agents, and as a result you may be receiving less-than-objective advice if the sponsoring company is recommended.

You might also refer to annuity and RRIF tables published in some daily newspapers that tell you what monthly income is currently available in return for $50,000 of RRSP funds. *The Toronto Star* publishes annuity tables with its Dollars & Sense column on the second Sunday of each month, and RRIF tables on the fourth Sunday.

Those of you with an insurance-company group RRSP available through your employer should ask the insurer involved to submit a quote on your annuity. Companies often offer a better rate to people who have already placed their money with them, whether in a group RRSP or an individual plan.

If you're leaning toward RRIFs, and you're interested in GICs or term deposits, check major daily newspapers for regular surveys. Remember you shouldn't compare RRIFs strictly on the basis of interest rates because of the importance of the contractual provisions. Don't ignore the varying methods of crediting interest. A published rate of 9 percent on a RRIF from one company may not provide the same income as 9 percent from another. Ask for a computer printout and compare the income streams. When it comes to self-directed RRIFs, you're going to want to ask more questions about fees, commissions and other charges.

Not only is shopping around for the best plan a wise move, it's equally important to know the person you'll be dealing with. He or she should be in a position to do business with a range of companies, and have the ability to handle the paperwork necessary to transfer your RRSP funds and implement your annuity and/or RRIF. Most people doing this won't charge for the paperwork. They're paid a commission by the financial institution offering the annuity or RRIF – and that's one reason it's important to obtain an unbiased survey comparing current quotations from competing companies.

For more on how your annuity or RRIF salesperson is paid, see chapter 33.

How to find a broker

Advisors come in all shapes and sizes. We've often referred in this book to broker/agents or annuity brokers. These people specialize in annuities and RRIFs, and earn most of their income dealing with people in their sixties or seventies.

If you live in a metropolitan area, you'll find these retirement income specialists listed under "annuities" in the Yellow Pages telephone directory. Better still, friends, relatives or even your employer may be able to recommend someone who has provided them with good service.

In smaller centres, a local insurance agent may have expertise in this area. The alternative is a bank or trust company, a few of which have specialists on staff to help people who are winding down RRSPs. However, most such transactions take place at the local branch level, where you are unlikely to find people with expertise in RRIFs and annuities. Most banks and trust companies offer only RRIFs, and are not fully conversant with annuities.

Keep in mind that the institution holding your RRSP funds will want to keep them there. There's nothing wrong with this – as long as you find a plan that fits your needs.

You should also take a long-term approach to choosing an advisor, especially if you opt for a RRIF or LIF that requires ongoing guidance. Consider the following types of advisors and salespeople:

A RRIF/annuity broker. These people have a variety of backgrounds, including life insurance and banking. Some will be chartered life underwriters, chartered financial planners, or chartered financial consultants.

- A life insurance agent or broker.
- A stockbroker.
- A bank, trust company or credit union manager.
- A chartered accountant (who may require the assistance of someone in one of the categories above to implement your plan).

CHAPTER 32

When and How to Make Your Purchase

ALTHOUGH THERE IS NOT AN ideal time to cash in your RRSP, we can suggest some guidelines that will help you determine the best time for you.

As we've already mentioned, you must wind up your RRSP by the end of the year in which you turn seventy-one. Whether you should wait that long is a question of financial need and of simple arithmetic. Clearly, a larger nest egg can be accumulated within a tax-sheltered investment than outside one. Holding off on the purchase of annuities or RRIFs, and hanging on to your tax-sheltered RRSP, is to your advantage because compound interest is on your side. But if you need the money, or simply want to enjoy the income your RRSP will produce, you have three choices: an annuity, a RRIF or cash withdrawals from your RRSP.

For many people, non-financial considerations outweigh the benefits of waiting until age seventy-one. For example, if you're sixty and want the money to travel while you have the vitality to enjoy it, income from your annuity or RRIF could be the answer.

Timing is crucial

Of course, you should buy a RRIF or annuity when interest rates are high. But how high is high? Kirk Polson told a client in early 1987 that interest rates were at a ten-year low, so perhaps the man should defer an annuity purchase unless he clearly needed the income. The response of this seventy-year-old was that 9 percent to 10 percent was high to someone who had lived through 4 percent, 5 percent and 6 percent interest in the 1950s and 1960s.

If you're concerned about rates, you may want to buy a series of annuities over a number of years to "average out" your investments. If you're putting your RRIF money into interest-bearing assets such as GICs or bonds, stagger the maturity dates in the RRIF.

Many people prefer to avoid having to make reinvestment decisions every year. If you're one of them, simply buy a five-year GIC or longer-term deposit for your RRIF. If you're under seventy-one and want to buy a RRIF, you don't have to commit all your RRSP money at once. Use part of the funds to buy a RRIF now, and add to it later, but before the end of your seventy-first year.

If you're sixty-five and have no employer pension, consider buying an annuity or RRIF right away so you don't waste the pension tax credit – a maximum of $170 federally ($200 in Quebec) if you have at least $1,000 of pension income. The credit, which directly reduces your tax, is further enhanced by a provincial addition to the federal portion. OAS and CPP retirement benefits don't qualify for this tax break.

When you retire or are approaching retirement, review RRSP maturity options and establish your financial requirements. Consider a deferred annuity that doesn't begin making payments until after you retire. This is especially advantageous if interest rates are high. Provided the general level of interest rates doesn't change, in most cases you can create a higher pension for yourself this way than by leaving your RRSP intact until retirement.

What if interest rates drop?

What if interest rates are down in the year you retire, but you need the income? Or interest rates are down when you turn seventy-one, but you're forced by government rules to make a decision?

In this situation, one of the best strategies is to arrange a short-term RRIF. For example, you could set up a RRIF holding a one-year guaranteed investment certificate and hope that rates rise by renewal time. While no one can know where interest rates will be when you renew, you will have avoided locking in your money for a long term at low yields.

Or suppose you feel current interest rates are high and you want to lock in those rates. You may be retiring in a few years or close to age seventy-one. How can you guarantee those rates? Consider a deferred or prepaid RRIF, a vehicle currently available from six life insurance companies: Canada Life, Great-West Life, North American Life, Royal Life, Standard Life and Manulife Financial.

The deferred or prepaid RRIF is actually a deferred term-certain annuity to age ninety that has a valuable option. It allows you to lock in interest rates for fifteen to thirty years with the ability to convert the annuity to a RRIF no later than the end of your seventy-first year. Because the annuity is deferred, you do not draw any income – your money accumulates at the guaranteed interest rate just as it would in a RRSP. When you require income you make the conversion to a RRIF and select the amount of income you need.

Let's take an example. Assume you are sixty years old and have $50,000 in your RRSP. You opt for the prepaid RRIF and select an investment term of fifteen years, yielding 8.875 percent in July, 1994. Under the terms of the plan your money will accumulate at 8.875 percent (compounded annually as it would in an RRSP) until the end of your seventy-first year, eleven years in this example.

On or before that date, you can take the guaranteed annuity income or convert to a RRIF. If you convert to a RRIF, your plan would earn the same interest for the remaining four years of the original fifteen-year term. It would then renew at prevailing interest rates at the end of the fifteen years.

Since you are able to guarantee interest rates for fifteen to thirty years under this prepaid RRIF, this plan is only for people who are prepared to make a long-term commitment. Interest rates vary with the term chosen and the amount of your investment. You avoid the necessity of continually reinvesting term deposits. Although the prepaid RRIF is cashable, interest penalties may apply if you decide to bail out at a later date. Generally, the companies offering the prepaid RRIF have no set-up or annual administration fees. Each company offers a variety of RRIF pay-out alternatives, but some plans are more flexible than others.

One thing that should be obvious is that you can't arrange your annuity or RRIF until your RRSP proceeds are available. If you're in a non-redeemable RRSP for a fixed term, you can't use the money to buy an annuity or RRIF until the end of that term.

Unfortunately, as already mentioned, the renewal periods for RRSPs don't necessarily coincide with your income needs. If you know you're going to wait until age seventy-one, it's simple to arrange to have your RRSPs mature that year. If you're in your sixties and can't be certain about future requirements, what can you do?

First, you must think about when you'll need income each time you renew your RRSPs. Then you'll be able to plan your investments so they are available when you need them. Then, assuming your RRSP funds are at your disposal, buy an annuity and/or RRIF at least six to eight weeks before you want the first cheque.

Financial institutions move in and out of the annuity and RRIF market according to investment opportunities. Once you sign a contract, the quoted rate is generally good for twenty-one to sixty days, depending on the company. This means your RRSP money must be made available during this period or the quotation is not binding.

Transfers take time

You've likely read newspaper horror stories about how long it can take to transfer money between financial institutions. These transfers are done on a tax-free, "rollover" basis that requires the use of government forms. Revenue Canada Form T2033 is used for transferring money between RRSPs or from an RRSP to an annuity or RRIF. Some financial institutions will transfer funds quickly, in two or three days. Others take as long as four or five weeks. What is needed is an accountable system under which your RRSP can be transferred electronically between institutions within a specific time frame.

If you deal with a specialist, you'll find that the average time lag is about ten days. Annuity/RRIF brokers handle these transactions daily, and are familiar with the financial institutions' procedures. Brokers are also interested in expediting the process because they don't get paid until the money is transferred.

At particular times of the year, such as the February RRSP deposit rush, financial institutions tend to put redemptions on the back burner for a few weeks. As a result, they often need prodding to move quickly. And if your RRSP money is in a mutual fund, you may have to wait until the valuation date – which could be daily, weekly or even the end of the month – to redeem your units.

It's not necessary for you to involve yourself in these procedures if you have a RRIF/annuity broker acting for you. In addition, if you have a number of RRSPs becoming available within a month or two, it's also unnecessary for you to take the trouble of consolidating them into one RRSP. This is a chore your broker can handle.

On the other hand, you can get involved if you wish. The simplest way is to take a completed Revenue Canada T2033 form to the institution holding your RRSP and let it be known that you want to pick up a cheque for the redemption proceeds on a particular date.

To qualify as a tax-free direct transfer, the cheque must be made out to the institution that will provide your RRIF or annuity income. Once the money is transferred, you will receive a signed trust agreement or a RRIF or annuity policy within a few weeks. If a life insurance broker/agent or an annuity/RRIF broker is involved, he will likely receive the documents and forward them to you.

As with insurance policies, these documents are important because they spell out the provisions of your annuity or RRIF. Future changes you may want to make, such as designating a beneficiary, will require an endorsement (an add-on to the contract).

In setting up your RRIF or annuity, the company will need the following information and documents to process your application:

- The account number for each RRSP and the names and addresses of the companies holding them;
- Your social insurance number;
- Your birth certificate;
- Details of your banking arrangements.

The same information may also be required from your spouse.

CHAPTER 33

How Annuity/RRIF Salespeople Are Paid

HOW MUCH IS THE PERSON who sells you an annuity or RRIF paid? Who pays him? Can you get a better deal by going directly to the company selling the product rather than dealing through a broker?

These are interesting questions, and ones you should know the answers to before you go shopping for your retirement investments.

First, the commission is paid entirely by the financial institution that sells the annuity or RRIF. Some banks market RRIFs too, but they generally don't sell through brokers.

Whether you deal directly with the insurance or trust company or through a RRIF/annuity broker, the compensation to the salesperson is the same. That's why it makes sense to buy through someone who will shop for you.

With annuities, there is only the commission to consider, and no extra fees. The commission is built into the annuity you buy and is paid to the broker or insurance company agent. However, some RRIFs come with setup charges or other administration fees, so inquire.

Annuity commissions range from about 1.5 percent to 3 percent of the amount invested. Larger commissions, in percentage terms, are paid on smaller amounts in recognition of the fact that a small sale is likely to involve as much work as a larger one. Typically, the commission is 3 percent on a $25,000 annuity, 2.5 percent to 3 percent on $50,000 to $75,000, 2 percent on $100,000 and as little as 1.0 percent on larger amounts. With large annuities, a common variation of this commission structure is for the company to pay the broker 2.5 percent to 3 percent on the first $100,000 and up to 2 percent on the amount over $100,000.

When it comes to RRIFs, the method of paying an agent or broker can be quite different. This is because the underlying investments may be mutual funds, stocks or bonds – instead of just those based on interest rates.

With interest-bearing RRIFs, you can invest for periods of as little as one year or choose a term with a guaranteed interest rate to age ninety. If a sixty-five-year-old buys a RRIF with a rate guaranteed for twenty-five years to age ninety, the salesperson's commission is in the 2.5 percent to 3 percent range. If a short-term RRIF is chosen, the seller is paid a short-term commission, but gets the chance to earn more with each renewal. For a one-year term, the broker receives from 0.2 percent to 0.4 percent; for five years, 1 percent to 2 percent; for ten years, about 2 percent; and for 15 or more years, 2 percent to 3 percent. If you keep rolling over the RRIF every year or few years, the broker gets about the same total commission as he would on one long, guaranteed term.

You can also invest in a RRIF-eligible mutual fund through a stockbroker or mutual fund salesperson. Mutual funds often carry up-front "loads" of 1 percent to 4 percent, although some will charge as much as 9 percent while others charge nothing at all. Some funds are available with a deferred sales charge. These are fees charged if you redeem your units or shares within the first few years; some will charge a redemption fee for up to nine years from the original deposit. Ask about administration fees, which can be $25 a year or more, and management fees.

Finally, there are self-directed RRIFs that you can set up with investment dealers and some trust companies. Usually, you pay $100 annually to maintain a self-directed RRIF, plus the usual brokers' fees for stock transactions. But there are no charges for buying interest-bearing securities such as Canada Savings Bonds, treasury bills and guaranteed investment certificates.

A RRIF, unlike an annuity, may require continuing service and advice from a broker. If you aren't pleased with the service you receive, you can switch your RRIF to another broker. This may mean the original broker loses further commissions. The broker also loses if you cash a RRIF or annuity. In the end, your broker should work to keep you happy – and to keep the commissions you generate.

CHAPTER 34

Easing the Tax Blow at Retirement

IN THE YEAR IN WHICH YOU retire, it is quite possible that you will earn more money than in any previous or subsequent year, especially if you receive a lump-sum retirement allowance. Retirement allowances have become quite common, more so in the 1990s when many Canadian companies battling the recession are finding it economically sound to offer incentives to older employees to retire early.

Many people would pay an enormous amount of income tax on this once-in-a-lifetime jump in earnings if were not for provisions in the Income Tax Act – generous ones, too – that allow you to shelter large chunks of retirement allowances in RRSPs, even if this causes you to exceed the usual RRSP limits. Unfortunately, a benefit given with one hand is snatched away with the other; many people receiving retiring allowances are hit with the alternative minimum tax. This is a provision aimed at keeping the well-to-do from sheltering too much of their income from tax but it can catch others, too.

Before explaining the minimum tax, let's look at how the tax act spells relief when you retire. Then we'll look at an example of how one person who took early retirement in 1991 was able to save tax by knowing and using the rules.

The first and most significant tax break is the ability to move retirement allowances into an RRSP on a tax-deferred basis, within limits. The limit is $2,000 for each calendar year of employment in 1989 and subsequent years. For service prior to 1989, the limit is $2,000 for each calendar year plus $1,500 for each calendar year in which you did not belong to an employer's pension or deferred profit-sharing plan. (When rolling over the allowance into an RRSP, you can count a calendar year as less than twelve months. If you began working in October 1960, for example, you would count 1960 as a full year.)

It's advisable to have your employer transfer the money directly into your RRSP. Otherwise, you will have to pay withholding tax. If you have already received a retirement allowance this year and tax was withheld despite your intention to put the money in an RRSP, you will be able to claim the tax withheld on your next tax return.

If you will be in a lower tax bracket in retirement, you should consider asking your employer to delay payment of any part of the retirement allowance which cannot be rolled into an RRSP until the following January. If payment is delayed, the money will be considered by Revenue Canada to be income in that year – and it will be taxed at the lower rate.

If you receive pension or deferred profit-sharing plan income instead of (or in addition to) a lump-sum retiring allowance, you cannot transfer any of it into an RRSP. However, you are allowed to transfer up to $6,000 of this income into a spousal RRSP in any year up to and including 1994. A spousal RRSP is an RRSP which you establish for your spouse. It is quite separate from a plan he or she already owns, or might open in the future.

Finally, legal expenses incurred to collect a retirement allowance are deductible against the allowance, or against the pension income to which the expenses relate. They are not deductible against other income.

Let's get down to the example of how one Canadian who retired in 1991 was able to slash his tax bill by using these rules.

His lump-sum retirement allowance was $125,000, certainly a hefty sum, but not unusual for a senior employee with many years of service. If the man (let's call him Mr. Smart) had simply added this amount to his 1991 income, his income for that year from employment, interest, dividends and the Canada Pension Plan retirement benefit would have been $184,453. (You'll recall that the CPP retirement benefit is normally payable at age sixty-five but can be collected as early as age sixty if you "substantially retire" earlier. Mr. Smart, who had turned sixty in 1991, took this option.)

As a citizen of Ontario, Mr. Smart would have paid $76,986 tax on that income. Rather than bear that tax bite, Mr. Smart chose to tax-shelter as much income as possible by putting most of the retiring allowance into an RRSP. In fact, under the years-of-service limits, Mr. Smart could tax-shelter $97,500. He then decided to ask his employer not to pay the remaining $27,500 retirement allowance until January 1992 when his income, and tax bracket,

Whittling Down Your Retirement Tax Bill

This table illustrates the tax savings that can be enjoyed at retirement by taking advantage of the provisions in the Income Tax Act that allow you to shelter retirement allowances in RRSPs. In this example, the retirement allowance is $125,000 and the employee is allowed to roll $97,500 into an RRSP under the years-of-service limits.

Tax Scenario	1992 Tax	1993 Tax	Total Tax
Paying tax on $125,000 lump sum	$76,986	$7,238	$84,224
Rolling $97,500 into an RRSP and			
deferring receipt of $27,500 until 1992	$29,446	$6,607	$36,053
With 1992 $3,643 RRSP contribution	$29,446	$5,057	$34,503
With $6,000 spousal RRSP contribution	$29,446	$3,682	$33,128

TABLE XXXI

would drop dramatically. (Employers don't have to do this, but there is no harm asking.)

As you can see in Table XXXI, Mr. Smart slashed his 1991 income tax to $29,446 by taking these two steps. His financial advisor suggested that his anticipated tax bill for both years should be considered as a single total, since the income would be taxed partly in 1992 and partly in 1991.

It was calculated that Mr. Smart's tax in 1992 would be $6,607, for a total tax of $36,053 for 1991 and 1992. But that tax bill doesn't take into consideration Mr. Smart's 1991 RRSP contribution. Under the post-1990 retirement income rules (described in Chapter 10), Mr. Smart's maximum tax-deductible RRSP contribution for 1991 is $3,643. The extra deduction reduces Mr. Smart's 1992 tax from $6,607 to $5,057. The two-year total tax drops to $34,503.

This wasn't the end. Until 1994, Mr. Smart can transfer up to $6,000 a year of pension income to a spousal RRSP. Mr. Smart will have $8,800 of pension income in 1991 so he decided to open a spousal RRSP and contribute $6,000. The result: his 1992 tax is reduced to $3,682 and the 1991-92 total is $33,128.

Mr. Smart was able to reduce the tax bill for his retirement year by tax-sheltering the maximum allowable amount in an RRSP and deferring receipt of the rest until 1992. With those two steps he saved $47,540 in 1991 tax. By making the maximum RRSP contribution and putting as much as he could in a spousal RRSP as well, he trimmed his 1991-92 taxes by another $2,925.

Impressive, isn't it? We have just one more word of advice. If you have received or will receive a lump-sum payment in your retirement year, don't do the above sort of calculation yourself unless you're very clever with figures. There could be thousands of dollars at stake. Spend a few hundred to have a professional – an accountant, tax lawyer, financial planner or other professional advisor – do the number-crunching and prepare your tax returns for the year you retire and your first full year of retirement.

CHAPTER 35

Term Deposits, GICs and Cannie Maes

MOST RETIRED PEOPLE, AND those who are close to retirement, favour investments that are more conservative than they might have chosen earlier in life. That often means using RRSP savings to purchase guaranteed investments such as GICs, term deposits and "prescribed" annuities.

The following are some of the key points to keep in mind if you're investing in term deposits and GICs:

• GICs and term deposits are similar. But generally, GIC funds are locked in for one to five years and term deposits for thirty to 270 days.

• They're available from banks, trust companies and credit unions. Shop around to be sure you're getting the most for your money.

• Make sure your deposits are insured. The Canada Deposit Insurance Corp. provides up to $60,000 worth of protection for most deposits of up to five years' duration held in your name at each financial institution. That's apart from another $60,000 of deposits you may hold jointly with your spouse, and a further $60,000 that each of you may hold in RRSP and/or RRIF deposits at the same institution. Although credit unions aren't eligible for the federal insurance, provincial agencies provide parallel coverage.

• Your best bet is to stagger maturity dates so you always have some money becoming available each year. This way you can reinvest each deposit for five years, thus obtaining the highest interest rate, while having the assurance that one-fifth of your non-tax-sheltered money will be available every year for an emergency – or for planned spending. This means you won't have to dip into a RRIF and perhaps put your future retirement income at risk.

• Term deposits and GICs pay interest annually, semi-annually, quarterly or monthly. Before retirement, people tend to choose annual interest payments because they're earning salaries and don't need the regular cash flow from their investments. For retirees, monthly interest may be preferable, though you'll usually have to accept half a percentage point less in interest for the convenience.

• These types of deposits may be redeemable or non-redeemable.

• A redeemable deposit will allow you to get out before maturity, although you'll pay an interest-rate penalty of about half a percentage point.

• When Canada Savings Bonds are issued in late October and early November, many institutions offer GICs designed to compete with CSBs. You must usually keep them for at least sixty days before you receive any interest. Watch your local newspaper for a listing of interest rates on GICs and term deposits.

Life insurance companies are also becoming more aggressive in this market. They call their term deposits and GICs "deferred annuities," and usually they're available only from agents and brokers. (These deferred annuities are not to be confused with the deferred payout annuities of the single- and joint-life type discussed earlier for RRSP wind-downs.) Income from these insurance company plans qualifies for the pension income credit – an advantage if you don't have income from an employer pension. These plans work the same way as a bank or trust company certificate, but at some point – usually when you turn 90 or 100 – your term deposit will automatically be turned into a life annuity if you haven't moved the money out by that time.

An added attraction of the life insurance plans (the companies have long claimed) is that they may be creditor-proof simply by naming your spouse or your child as beneficiary. This could be an advantage for self-employed people. (However, a 1990 tax case in Saskatchewan may mean that these life insurance plans are not as creditor-proof as believed in specific situations.) Yet another advantage is avoidance of the delay caused by the probating of your will – but only if you have named a beneficiary. The insurance company pays the money directly to the named beneficiary, without the funds going through your estate. This could result in a substantial saving of probate fees; in Ontario, for example, this could amount to as much as $1,500 on a $100,000 deposit.

If you're not put off by the thought of giving up liquidity of your non-registered money, you might consider a life insurance company's "prescribed" annuity. With prescribed annuities, as you'll see in the next chapter, you give up control of your capital in return for a better after-tax return than those provided by GICs or term deposits.

Mortgage-backed securities

Mortgage-backed securities have been available for only a few years but they have found favour with older investors. Commonly known as Cannie Maes, they are a Canadian adaptation of the popular Ginnie Maes (derived from GNMA for Government National Mortgage Association) in the United States.

Mortgage-backed securities are pools of insured residential first mortgages issued by banks and trust companies in which you can invest as little as $5,000. As an investor in a mortgage-backed security, you are investing in securities made up of mortgages that have enabled people to buy homes.

People usually encounter mortgages as a debt they have had to pay as homeowners. As an investor in a mortgage-backed security, you are on the receiving side of a mortgage instead of the paying side.

Once you've invested in a Cannie Mae, you will receive a monthly income that is a blend of principal and interest. This income will last usually for five, but occasionally for ten years. At the end of the term of the Cannie Mae, you receive your original investment back, less any payments made on the principal over the years by the home-owners.

Cannie Maes come in both prepayable and non-payable forms. Because of the nature of a prepayable investment, your income from a Cannie Mae can go up and down. For example, some homeowners might begin paying off their mortgages more quickly, giving you more income as those mortgage prepayments flow through to the investors. If this is extra cash you don't need, you will be stuck reinvesting it, possibly at lower interest rates. When your Cannie Mae matures, you could receive less money than you had anticipated since more money will have been paid to you in the early years.

Your mortgage-backed security matures when the last underlying mortgage in the pool matures. However, you could sell your security before then. The federal government's Canada Mortgage and

Housing Corp. unconditionally guarantees that the interest and principal will be paid; this guarantee makes the investments virtually risk-free. As a result, there is a reasonably strong secondary market for Cannie Maes. If you do sell, the market value of your investment will depend on whether interest rates have risen or fallen since you bought the security. Just like a bond, a Cannie Mae will trade at a premium if it has a higher rate of interest than the prime mortgage rate and at a discount if it is paying less. However, a mortgage-backed security will provide a slightly higher yield than a government bond of the same maturity.

Mortgage-backed securities offer investors the advantage of monthly income, a federal government guarantee, a yield slightly higher than federal government bonds and the ability to sell at any time. They are also eligible for inclusion in self-administered RRSPs and RRIFs.

If you are interested in this investment, you should compare mortgage-backed securities with monthly interest GICs, even though the two investments differ somewhat, especially in the ease with which you can sell them if you need the cash. In mid-1994, the yield on a five-year Cannie Mae was 8.5 percent compared with 8.25 percent on five-year monthly interest GICs.

Cannie Maes are sold through investment houses. If you feel they should be part of your retirement income program, call your broker.

CHAPTER 36

Prescribed Annuities: Increasing Your Yield

TO CANADIANS IN THE HAPPY position of reaching age seventy-one with ample retirement savings, the RRSPs built up over many years suddenly have a downside. RRSPs must be converted into periodic retirement income – RRIFs, annuities or a combination of the two – by the end of the year in which the holder turns seventy-one.

This means the RRSP is gone forever, and so is a major opportunity to shelter income from tax. What can you do if you still have income that you want sheltered from tax? If you're willing to give up liquidity of some of your capital, you might try the prescribed annuity. In certain circumstances you can increase your after-tax investment income by 25 to 50 percent.

A prescribed annuity is a type of annuity that is purchased with money on which no tax is owed. This might be capital on which the tax has already been paid or on which it was never owed, such as proceeds from a life insurance policy or from the sale of a principal residence. A prescribed annuity results in a level blend of interest and principal, so payments are the same each month – much like a blended-payment home mortgage.

Only your interest is taxed

When you receive periodic payments under a prescribed annuity, you pay tax only on the interest generated by the capital. The older the purchaser, the greater the payout and the lower the tax. That's because the older person's life expectancy is shorter. As a result, you end up with more money in your pocket after tax than you would from term deposits or bonds. A prescribed annuity can be the life type (paid for life, or joint-life) or the term-certain type (to age ninety or for a shorter period).

Let's take the example of a man of seventy-five who has $50,000 of spare capital and wants to know whether to put it into a

Prescribed Annuities Versus GICs

MALE, AGE 75
$50,000 INVESTMENT
5-YEAR GIC YIELDING 8.0% MONTHLY
LIFE ANNUITY, MINIMUM 10 YEARS: $525.45 MONTHLY

	Prescribed Annuity	GIC
Monthly income	$ 525.45	$ 333.33
Total annual income	6,305.40	4,000.00
Tax-free portion	3,855.02	—
Taxable portion	2,450.38	4,000.00
Income tax payable at 40% marginal rate	980.15	1,600.00
Net disposable annual income	5,325.25	2,400.00

Note: The net disposable annual income under the prescribed annuity is equivalent to investing in a GIC yielding 17.8% for a person in a 40% marginal tax bracket.

TABLE XXXII

prescribed annuity or to invest in a five-year GIC yielding 8.0 percent monthly. Suppose that, instead of putting the $50,000 into a GIC, this person bought a single-life prescribed annuity with a ten-year guarantee. The annuity pays for life or, in the case of death within ten years, the rest of the money goes to heirs or the estate. See Table XXXII for the bottom-line results.

In this case, the $50,000 generates monthly income of $525.45, of which only $204.20 is taxable. In the 40 percent bracket, the prescribed annuity is generating after-tax income of $443.77. That's $243.77 more a month than with the GIC. With the GIC, the person would still have $50,000 in capital when the certificate matures in five years. On the other hand, the annuity guarantee means that the purchaser – or the heirs or estate – would benefit for at least ten years or $63,054. As mentioned previously, the downside of a prescribed annuity, and annuities in general, is the fact that you must give up liquidity of your capital. For some, this drawback will outweigh any yearly financial gain. If you just can't stomach the thought, consider an "insured" prescribed annuity.

If you're a non-smoker in good health, you may be able to guarantee the tax-free return of your capital to your estate at death by using a life annuity and an insurance policy – and still have

"Insured" Prescribed Annuities Versus GICs

MALE, AGE 75 (NON-SMOKER)
$50,000 INVESTMENT
5-YEAR GIC YIELDING 8.0% MONTHLY
LIFE ANNUITY, NO GUARANTEE
$50,000 LIFE INSURANCE POLICY

	Prescribed Annuity	GIC
Monthly income	$ 621.35	$ 333.33
Total annual income	7,456.20	4,000.00
Tax-free portion	4,683.89	—
Taxable portion	2,772.31	4,000.00
Income tax payable at 40% marginal rate	1,108.92	1,600.00
Net annual income	6,347.28	2,400.00
Less annual insurance cost	(2,973.00)	—
Net disposable annual income	3,374.28	2,400.00

Your original investment of $50,000 is returned to your estate on death. The net disposable annual income under the prescribed annuity is equivalent to investing in a GIC yielding 11.25% assuming a 40% marginal tax bracket.

TABLE XXXIII

more left after tax than with a term deposit. Refer to Table XXXIII. In this second example, the seventy-five year old man has a monthly lifetime income of $621.35. This income stops on death, but at that time his original investment of $50,000 is returned tax-free to his beneficiary. (Probate fees can be avoided on death if your spouse or children are named on the life insurance policy as beneficiary.)

Most of you could enjoy the income advantages of the insured annuity with the plus of having your capital returned to your family on death, regardless of how long you live. Keep in mind that the annuity cannot be cashed at a later date, so consider the insured annuity for part of your investment portfolio, keeping other money liquid. Although the advantage of prescribed annuities increases with age, they are also useful for younger people, thanks to changes announced in 1987. Until then, a person had to be disabled or at least sixty years old to be eligible for a prescribed annuity. Now anyone can purchase one.

CHAPTER 37

There's No Place Like Home

IT REALLY IS TRUE. THERE IS no place like your home for family memories, personal satisfaction and financial reward. For people approaching retirement, the house, condominium, co-op apartment or cottage bought many years ago is usually paid for and has been appreciating in value for most of the years you've owned it.

Moreover, providing it's your principal residence, not a secondary home, you can sell your home and pocket all those years of gain tax-free. You may, in fact, have been planning all along to do exactly that – turning in your big, rambling family house for a smaller, less expensive house or apartment, perhaps in a location where inflation hasn't hit as hard as in the cities. In that case, you'll want to know the principal residence rules so that you can get maximum benefit from this huge tax advantage.

On the other hand, perhaps you're like many older Canadians – house-rich and cash-poor. It is estimated that seniors own about a million homes in Canada, and that more than 40 percent of these people have annual incomes of less than $15,000. They're often sitting on hundreds of thousands of dollars of equity, but if they sold their homes, which they're usually reluctant to do, they'd only have to turn around and pay for comparable shelter elsewhere. For people in this bind, the answer may be the reverse mortgage, a recent product in Canada that allows you to tap into your equity without selling your home.

Let's start with the principal residence rules. If you own one home that you normally inhabit, even a mobile home or boat, it is exempt from capital gains tax. Whether it's valued at $1 million or $20,000, if you sell it you will enjoy a total exemption from the appreciation in value for the years you have owned it. You can then buy another, perhaps smaller, home and enjoy the same tax advantage.

If you rent your home in the city but own a cottage, chalet or other vacation property, it can be your principal residence for tax purposes. The exemption from capital gains tax on principal residences is in addition to the $100,000 lifetime capital gains exemption that each of us is allowed on any capital property.

This exemption was eliminated on February 22, 1994. However, qualifying gains up to that date will be eligible for exemption provided an election is filed with your 1994 tax return. By filing an election you are triggering any accrued capital gains. In other words, you will be treated as if you had sold the asset and immediately rebought it. The election is available for assets such as stocks and mutual funds and the portion of real estate gains, including those on your cottage, that are eligible for exemption under rules introduced in the 1992 federal budget.

By "crystallizing" (as this technique is known) capital gains accrued to the budget date, you are avoiding tax in the future when you sell the property or die. Following the death of both spouses or a single person you are deemed to have sold capital assets. This can present a problem if the asset, perhaps a cottage, is to be kept in the family. Your children will have to come up with cash to pay any tax on capital gains.

Are there any pitfalls to crystallizing capital gains? Yes. First, it is possible that even though you may get away without paying any tax on capital gains, you may find that you have to pay what is called alternative minimum tax (AMT). This is a tax that might be charged in the year the exemption is claimed and for which you could receive credit in future years when your income is lower. Second, the gain is added into your regular income for calculating the OAS clawback; so it is possible you could lose some or all of your OAS benefits by making the election.

Because of the importance of the election and some of the complications that can result, it might make sense for you to have an accountant assist with your 1994 income tax return. If you think you might elect to crystallize your gains, it would also be wise to determine the value of your property on February 22 as soon as possible. This could be difficult to do if you wait until you begin preparing your tax return.

You should note that prior to 1982, one spouse could claim a city home as a principal residence and the other could claim the family cottage for an exemption from capital gains tax on both properties.

The capital gains exemption on residences is limited to one for each family from that time on. However, the seemingly simple principal residence rules are complicated by the fact that the old rules continue to apply on your residences during the years prior to 1982. When you throw in the joint ownership and begin looking at who provided the money for the purchase, principal residence questions can get tangled indeed. To give you a flavour for what's involved, here are a few scenarios and how they could be resolved in specific instances.

Question: You and your wife have a house as well as a cottage, both bought twenty years ago. The properties were originally jointly owned; you provided the money to buy both homes. In 1978 you switched legal ownership of the house into your name and the cottage into her name. You now plan to sell the cottage. What's your capital gains position?

Answer: Because your wife assumed 100 percent ownership of the cottage, she can claim it as her principal residence until the end of 1981. When the cottage is sold, there will be a taxable capital gain, of which 75 percent is included in income, on the increase in value between Dec. 31, 1981 and the date of sale. Because you provided the money to buy the cottage, this capital gain is taxable to you, even though the cottage is in your wife's name. Your $100,000 lifetime capital gains exemption can be used to wipe out or reduce your capital gains liability by making an election in your 1994 income tax return, provided you haven't already used it. If you sell your house, it will be tax-free because you have had an ownership interest throughout.

Question: Apart from my principal residence, I have a second house that used to be my principal residence but is now rented out. Can I pay the tax on the capital gain that has accrued in the meantime? Then I won't have such a big bill to pay when I sell the house ten years from now. Should I if I can?

Answer: You can pay the tax owing or wait until you sell the house. Assuming houses will continue to increase in value over the long term, you may be better off waiting. If postponed, the tax will be calculated using a formula that takes into account the increase in value and the number of years that the property was taxable. Despite the advantage of tax deferral, if you still have all or most of your $100,000 capital gains exemption, some financial advisors suggest you trigger the tax in 1994. You can use your exemption to eliminate or reduce your tax bill.

Question: You and your parents are equal owners of a condominium that is your, not your parents', principal residence. A spare bedroom is rented out. What is your position if the capital gains are crystallized or the property is sold? Can your parents claim the borrowing costs on their investment?

Answer: Dealing first with capital gains, let's say the purchase price was $150,000 and the condo is eventually sold for $250,000, leaving a $100,000 profit to be shared, $50,000 to you and $50,000 to your parents. Because renting a room doesn't affect your principal residence status as long as you don't claim capital cost allowance, your entire gain will be tax-free. Since your parents don't live in the condo, they can't claim the principal residence exemption on their $50,000 gain. The accrued gain would still be exempt for them if each has $25,000 of their personal capital gains exemption still unused. Rental income, mortgage interest and running expenses for the rented part of the condo would be reported equally by you and your parents. If your parents borrowed the money to buy into the property, the interest would be deductible as an investment expense.

Question: You and your spouse have jointly owned and lived on a farm for twenty years. Each of you contributed equally to its purchase. In the past five years, the property has developed into a cash-crop enterprise, with income reported jointly. You both have your lifetime capital gains exemptions intact. What's your capital gains position if you sell?

Answer: Your capital gains on farms depend on the zoning. Rural jurisdictions might specify the zoning of, say, ten-acre lots, as residential properties. In this case, the full ten acres would qualify for the principal residence exemption. Other areas zone only one-acre lots as residential. In this case, the house and up to an acre of land would qualify for the principal residence exemption. The rest of the farm would then be a "qualified farm property" eligible for a special $500,000 capital gains exemption. Since there are two $500,000 exemptions to take into account, yours and your spouse's, there would be no capital gains tax unless the farm, apart from the house and its adjoining acre, sells for more than $1 million.

As for the mechanics of claiming the principal residence exemption, it's done on Revenue Canada form T2091, which you file with your tax return for the year when you sell your home. There's no need to file the form if the gain is exempt, only if it's partly taxable, but you might have to fill out the form just to be sure you're completely exempt. For information on the principal residence exemption, obtain the Revenue Canada interpretation bulletin, IT-120R3, and the Capital Gains Tax Guide from your district taxation office.

However, many thousands of dollars could be at stake and a do-it-yourself analysis is no substitute for the guidance of a lawyer or accountant.

Finally, there's an intriguing and little-known facet to the principal residence exemption that could generate thousands of dollars for you – at least if you live in a big city where house inflation has been strongest. As mentioned, if you sell your principal residence and buy another, your gain on the first home is tax-free and your principal residence status will then apply on your new home. Further, if you move out of the first home without selling it, intending to rent it out, there is normally a deemed disposition of the property at fair market value and the tax-free capital appreciation under the principal residence exemption ends.

However, if you move out of your house without selling it and into an apartment, as many seniors do, you can benefit from up to five more years of capital appreciation. You have to make what the Income Tax Act calls a change-of-use election for the year you move out and there is no deemed disposition. The house can continue to qualify as your principal residence for four years, in some cases up to five. If you sell it after then, you will still enjoy any increase in value during those four or five years tax-free.

There isn't a Revenue Canada form for making the change-of-use designation. Instead, you must include a letter with your income tax return for the year you move out of your home. Describe the property and indicate that you're electing to make a change-of-use election under Section 45(2) of the Income Tax Act.

There is a downside to this strategy, but it isn't often significant: you'll have to pay income tax on the rental income you get from your house at the same time you'll be paying your own apartment rent with after-tax dollars. This might be balanced by the fact that you'll be able to deduct the property taxes on your rented-out home, plus any repairs and maintenance. Though you could claim capital cost allowance (depreciation) on your rented-out house, you might want to consider not doing so since you would just have to pay it back to Revenue Canada (a so-called "recapture") when the house is sold. On the other hand, if you are going to own the property for many years, it might be preferable to claim the allowance.

Reverse mortgages

Sometimes called equity conversion or home income plans, reverse mortgages were available from only a few financial institutions at the time of writing but major financial institutions were watching the concept carefully. The reverse mortgage is an insurance company product that gives homeowners the chance to tap into the equity they have in their homes and to enhance their income without having to sell their homes.

Here's how it works: you take out a mortgage on your home and the proceeds are used to buy an annuity that provides you with an income stream that is monthly, semi-annually or annually for life or for a fixed term. It's your choice. You can also opt for a lump sum. The income is not taxable. For as long as you live in your home, you don't have to make monthly payments on the mortgage. Instead, this is what typically happens:

- If one spouse dies, the annuity payments continue to the other spouse. This may be the full amount or less, depending on the annuity option you chose.
- When the second spouse dies, the mortgage becomes due. If the home is sold, the company is repaid from the proceeds. Depending on how long the mortgage has existed, there may also be an early-withdrawal fee.
- If you have willed the home to your children or other beneficiaries, they may be able to take over the mortgage. They would have to meet the usual qualifications and, as the new owners of the home, start repaying the company through conventional mortgage payments. As with other annuities, you can choose among features that include inflation indexing and a guarantee period. If you have a fifteen-year guarantee and both of you die within ten years, the commuted value of five years of further payments would be available to your heirs. A guarantee period is a must. Without it, the company would end up with a large chunk of your money if you died prematurely.

Let's take a look at an example. Say you live in a major metropolitan centre and your home is valued at $300,000. You and your spouse are both seventy years old. One financial institution would allow you a maximum mortgage of $94,100, a little over 30 percent of the value of your home. This would purchase a tax-free monthly income of $710.96 (in July 1993) payable for life on a joint-and-last-survivor basis.

The mortgage rate is 11.35 percent, roughly 3 percent more than the underlying interest assumptions in the annuity. Assuming the value of your home increases at 5 percent a year, it will be worth $488,668 at age eighty while the amount owing under the mortgage will be $283,815. Your equity in your home will be the difference, $204,854. Under the same assumptions you will still have equity in your home until age eighty-nine, at which age the mortgage will exceed the value of the home.

The annuity payments that are integral to the reverse mortgage qualify for coverage of up to $2,000 a month under the insurance industry's consumer protection plan, set up in January 1990, to compensate people if a life insurer becomes insolvent. The maximum reverse mortgage depends on the homeowners' ages, the location (you don't have much chance to get one if you live in a depressed area), the home's appraised value and prevailing interest rates.

A reverse mortgage may seem intimidating but there are several benefits. The most obvious is that you continue to live in your own home and enjoy an adequate income. Second, because you have not sold your home, you continue to benefit from appreciation in value.

Before proceeding with a reverse mortgage, review your complete financial picture with an independent financial advisor. Make certain your income-producing assets are generating the maximum income with the minimum tax. Only then should you consider a reverse mortgage. Recognize that the transaction will bring a significant financial reward for the reverse mortgage salesperson, sometimes as much as 3 to 4 percent of the mortgage. Obtain a second opinion if you feel it is necessary. This is the house that you worked for and lived in for many years. You'll want to be certain a reverse mortgage is the best solution to your needs.

There's an application fee, plus the usual legal fees associated with any mortgage. Your home will have to be appraised and you should get independent legal advice.

CHAPTER 38

UI Benefits
after Age 65

ROUGH JUSTICE FOR PEOPLE in their sixties who aren't ready for retirement or cannot afford it has recently been won in two unrelated court decisions.

In a landmark decision in 1990, the Supreme Court of Canada ruled that employer's policies of mandatory retirement at age sixty-five are not unconstitutional. The closely watched ruling came at a time when companies were reducing staff, and it gave them the moral backing to ease older employees out the door.

The other court ruling had come earlier. A Quebec woman had gone to court to argue that it was unconstitutional under the Charter of Rights and Freedoms to be denied continuing unemployment coverage under the Unemployment Insurance Act simply because she had turned sixty-five. In 1988 an appeal court ruled that she was right, and the federal government decided to amend the UI legislation to reflect the ruling.

As a result of the two constitutional decisions, there are more older Canadians looking for work in the early 1990s in an economy that is still far from robust. At the same time Canada's social security net has been widened to accommodate an expanded need.

To understand the impact of the change, let's look at the UI rules before and after the amendment. Before November 18, 1990, employed people stopped paying UI premiums at age sixty-five and became ineligible for benefits. At that time, they were entitled to claim from Employment and Immigration Canada a lump sum equal to three weeks' unemployment benefits, if they had worked at least twenty weeks in the previous year whether or not they continued working. They had no further involvement with UI after that.

When the government moved to make working people eligible for unemployment benefits beyond age 65, the change became part of a rewriting of the UI rule book. Among other things, the lump sum at age sixty-five was abolished – as were the government's contributions to the UI program. The UI program is now financed entirely by employers and employees.

Not only can seniors receive UI benefits. The rules are the same as for anyone else. Eligibility for UI benefits for people of any age depends on continuing availability for work and the UI premiums paid in the last fifty-two weeks. On a sliding scale, the qualifying period ranges from twenty weeks in regions where the unemployment rate is 6 percent or less to as little as ten weeks where the rate is over 15 percent.

You must report all of your earnings while receiving UI benefits, but you are allowed to earn up to 25 percent of the weekly unemployment benefit before your benefit is reduced. Any earnings above the 25 percent or received during the two-week period between applying for benefits and payments beginning will be deducted from the benefits. Employment and Immigration has a definition of earnings that will be of particular interest to seniors. Among the "earnings" that you must report are pension income (we'll come to an important exception in a moment), Old Age Security payments, Canada Pension Plan benefits, self-employment earnings and damages for wrongful dismissal. The following sources of income do not count as earnings for UI purposes and should not be reported: income from personal RRSPs, annuities and RRIFs; disability pensions; and survivor's or dependent's pensions.

An employer pension will not be deducted from UI benefits in the following situation. Suppose you retire from Company A and start receiving your pension before you are hired by Company B. If you are laid off and make a UI claim based on your Company B job, your Company A pension will not be deducted from benefits.

The maximum UI disability benefit in 1994 is $429 a week. However, many claimants are not entitled to that much because they have worked in jobs in which the UI premium is less than the maximum. You can receive the unemployment benefit for up to fifty weeks following the two-week waiting period. There is no longer any age limit for claiming it. UI benefits are taxable.

To receive more information or apply for UI benefits, contact your local Canada Employment Centre, listed under E in the blue Government of Canada pages at the back of the phone book.

CHAPTER 39

Passing on Your Wealth

IF YOU ASK A GROUP OF people about their plans for passing on their wealth after their death, you'll probably be given three different kinds of answers.

Many people who have lived through the Great Depression are dedicated savers. They find it difficult to spend and they plan to leave as much as possible to their families. At the other end of the spectrum are the people who will tell you, "I'd like to spend my last dollar on the day I die." In the middle are those who are trying to maintain their pool of savings while living on their earnings.

Whatever your plans, if you don't take the time to organize your estate carefully, they're not likely to be fulfilled. But what exactly is estate planning? You should look at estate planning as long-range personal planning aimed at ensuring that your assets and earnings do you the most good while you're alive and your heirs the most good after you die.

While estate planning normally focusses on death, it can, and should, also involve a lifetime program to maximize savings and minimize income tax.

Estate planning is like an X-ray. Your financial health may appear fine on the surface, but an X-ray may uncover problems. This chapter will pinpoint those potential problems so that you and your advisors can correct them before it's too late.

It is normal and understandable to be reluctant to talk about passing on your wealth. No one likes to talk about "death" planning. It's not uncommon for someone to feel that his or her estate is simply not large enough to necessitate serious planning.

Furthermore, since the fruit of your efforts may not be obvious until after death, there is often a feeling that everything will take care of itself; there is a sense that there is no need to spend time and money bothering with these things now.

Another common objection to sitting down and planning is a belief that your lawyer or accountant is taking care of it. Unless you have specifically asked these people to address your concerns, it's unlikely they have done so.

Who should sit down and work out a plan for passing on their wealth? Everyone. Why? For a number of reasons, some of them more important for some people than for others. For example, you will want to ensure that there is enough cash available at death to pay any taxes and debts. Second, you will want to conserve your wealth by keeping as much of it as legally possible out of the tax-man's outstretched hands.

Third, estate planning often involves an attempt to provide a fair distribution of assets to a number of beneficiaries. Take, for instance, the business owner who has three children, only one of whom is involved in the business. It might naturally follow that the child active in the business will take over running the company after the parent's death, but what about the other children?

Finally, estate planning can involve the creation of wealth, often through life insurance.

Your advisors, as you plan for the passing on of your wealth, can come in various guises. In a straightforward situation, all you may need is a lawyer to draw up a will. In other situations, it might be advisable to bring in an accountant, a life insurance salesperson, a trust officer, a stockbroker or any other people you rely on for advice, including family members.

One way to understand what happens to your various assets upon your death is to imagine a funnel. Each of us can have four different types of assets: personal, business, life insurance and benefits provided by government programs. At death, all these assets become part of our estate. Personal assets pass to our heirs by will or by deed. Business assets – any business owned wholly or jointly with others – pass by will or through written agreement to business associates. The proceeds of life insurance policies go into your estate or directly to beneficiaries named in the policy.

Government benefits, such as the Canada Pension Plan lump-sum death benefit, go into the estate.

So estate planning is like pouring water into a funnel. The flared part at the top collects the water and directs it into the constricted neck of the funnel. It then goes through a filter and emerges at the

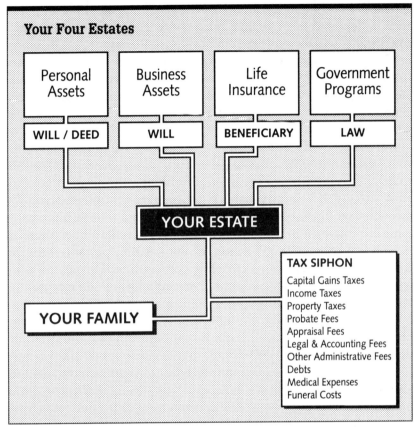

Your Four Estates

Personal Assets	Business Assets	Life Insurance	Government Programs
WILL / DEED	WILL	BENEFICIARY	LAW

YOUR ESTATE

TAX SIPHON

Capital Gains Taxes
Income Taxes
Property Taxes
Probate Fees
Appraisal Fees
Legal & Accounting Fees
Other Administrative Fees
Debts
Medical Expenses
Funeral Costs

YOUR FAMILY

CHART III

bottom. With our estate funnel, the value of what flows into your estate is not necessarily what flows out for your family.

You see, your estate funnel has its own filter. Various taxes, fees, expenses and debts associated with settling your estate have to be paid. They are filtered out. Don't be too concerned. After all, Canada doesn't have estate taxes at death. But don't get the impression that you'll avoid taxes altogether. There will be income taxes to be paid by your estate on income you earned that year to the date of your death. Also, and this is not so commonly known, any accrued capital gain has to be reckoned with at that time as well.

The government deems you to have disposed of all capital property (property that can increase in value), both depreciable and non-depreciable, immediately before death. The increase in value is potentially subject to tax at the capital gains rate of 75 percent and must be reported on your final income tax return. That could mean your estate owes a sizable sum to Revenue Canada.

There are exceptions. All capital property can be transferred to your spouse without paying tax at that time. This doesn't eliminate the tax, it simply defers it until your spouse dies and leaves the remaining assets to someone else, perhaps your children. The tax must then be paid.

Any capital gain accrued up to budget day 1994 is eligible for your lifetime $100,000 capital gains exemption, so, as discussed in chapter 38, it is wise to consider crystallizing the accrued gain in 1994. Finally, if you own shares in a Canadian-controlled, privately owned, small-business corporation, or if you are transferring qualifying farming operations to your children or grandchildren, there is a $500,000 exemption. For most of you, capital property will be confined to holding shares of public corporations. For people who own both a home and a cottage, tax on capital gains can represent a large potential tax liability.

As already mentioned, this tax liability does not arise until both husband and wife have died. If you are single, widowed or divorced, however, the tax becomes payable on your death.

Consider the case of someone in Ontario, where both residential and cottage property values increased dramatically in the late 1980s and early 1990s. Let's say you own a cottage within commuting distance of Toronto that was worth $30,000 in 1972, the year the capital gains tax came into effect. Today, after rapid growth in value, it is worth $250,000. In other words, a capital gain of $220,000 has accrued so far.

Before 1982, one spouse could claim the home as a principal residence and the other could claim the cottage, ensuring a total exemption from capital gains tax on the two properties. The rules now limit the capital gains exemption to one principal residence for a family. However, the old rules still apply up to 1982 for real estate bought earlier and still owned by the same people.

Consider a cottage that is not subject to the principal residence exemption. In 1994, if the spouse who owns it sells it, gives it to the children, or dies, and has not used the capital gains exemption, the first $100,000 of the gain will be tax-free, subject to the required election. However, the exemption will be restricted on real estate purchased before March 1992.

In our example, this means that 75 percent of $120,000 ($250,000 minus $30,000 minus $100,000) will be declared as income. This comes to $90,000, on which tax will have to be paid.

Your estate might also be reduced by any estate tax on assets in the United States (see Chapter 40). U.S. assets for estate purposes include not only real estate but U.S. stocks, bonds and other securities (but not bank accounts) and U.S. businesses owned personally as partnerships or proprietorships. Estate tax rates range from 18 percent on taxable estates worth $10,000 U.S. or less to 55 percent on amounts exceeding $3 million. There is a $60,000 exemption, but if you own a U.S. property jointly with your spouse, there is not a provision for deferring the tax until your spouse dies unless he or she is a U.S. citizen. U.S. estate tax is not creditable against Canadian income tax and vice versa. If you have a significant accrued gain on a U.S. property when you die you might end up paying Canadian income tax on the capital gains plus U.S. estate tax on the market value of the asset.

In the Canadian situation described earlier, and for those of you who own property in the United States, it's best to seek the advice of a tax accountant or tax lawyer to determine if there are any options available to you that can minimize or defer the potential tax liability.

As for RRSPs and annuities, please review earlier chapters which discuss the tax treatment of these assets. Generally, if there is no surviving spouse, the value of these items is fully taxable (that is, not as a capital gain but as income) in the year of death.

Many of you will take the approach that, regardless of taxes, fees or expenses that have to be paid at death, your family will inherit a generous sum and that, therefore, no further action is necessary. Others will recognize that if the estate contains little or no cash to pay potential tax liabilities, some assets will have to be sold.

Unfortunately in this situation, timing is everything. Market or economic conditions could make it inappropriate to sell the assets immediately after your death. Furthermore, there can be a great deal of sentimental value to the asset, especially a cottage, you leave behind and you may prefer that it remain in the family after your death.

What can you do? One alternative, if you're insurable, is to take out a life insurance policy that will provide enough cash to meet the tax liability at your death or at the death of both you and your spouse.

This kind of life insurance, known as a joint second-death policy, insures both husband and wife, providing a tax-free death benefit to the family or estate after both spouses have died. It is less expensive than a policy insuring one person and is an effective source of cash to pay taxes that become due when both spouses have died. It preserves the value of the estate and avoids a forced sale of assets to meet the tax bill.

Surprisingly enough, joint second-death policies of the term-insurance-to-age-100 type can be relatively inexpensive if you are in good health, particularly if you and your spouse don't smoke. Get your insurance broker or agent to obtain competitive quotations because premiums can vary considerably. Don't assume you won't qualify just because you're in your sixties. Few people are rejected outright, and some companies will issue a policy even if one person of the couple is uninsurable.

There's no arguing, though, that life insurance gets more expensive with advancing years. Of course, life insurance bought to pay taxes at death is above and beyond what you have provided for your spouse's needs in the event that you die first. While it's easy to figure out how much your spouse would need to live on, it's more difficult to get a handle on what your final tax bill will be. After all, you don't know how long you will live, how the tax rules will change or how much your cottage and other capital property will be worth at your death.

While it would be ideal if you could increase this insurance periodically to account for inflation, as you do with your home insurance, older people run into the expense barrier. You have to buy now all the insurance that might be needed for a tax bill some years away. About all you can do is make your best guess on what the amount will be, and err on the side of generosity. Your surviving spouse, after all, might have a problem if you don't buy enough insurance but won't if you buy too much.

At present, a non-smoking man, age fifty, could buy $250,000 of term-to-100 insurance for about $200 a month. On a joint last-life basis, if we assume his wife is the same age and a non-smoker, the monthly premium for the same amount of insurance (payable on the second death) would be about $74.

You can't pass on your wealth effectively without a will. Yet many people postpone making a will until it's too late. In this situation, the government of your province has rules on the disposition of your estate, but they are not likely to be completely in tune with your wishes. Furthermore, since you have not chosen anyone to administer your estate, there is a delay and additional cost until a court appoints an administrator.

To make a valid will, you must be "of sound mind" and be familiar with the act governing wills where you live, the extent of your assets and the identity of family members and friends who should be considered as potential beneficiaries. A will has no effect until death, and can be changed as often as you wish.

In fact, your will should be reviewed every three to five years to ensure that it still reflects your intentions and whenever major events in your life occur, such as the birth of children, the death of a spouse and a change in marital status. It is vital to rewrite your will if you remarry because marriage automatically revokes an existing will. You will also want to revise your will if you become separated and begin a common-law relationship. Jointly held property passes to the other owner without being specified in your will. Similarly, life insurance and RRSPs go to the beneficiaries.

One of the most important decisions in planning your will is choosing an executor. The executor plays an important role, identifying the assets in your estate, putting a value on them and distributing them to the beneficiaries. This person meets immediately after your death with family members and other interested people to discuss funeral arrangements and the provisions of the will.

If necessary, he confers with lawyers about representing the estate and other legal matters. Your executor also arranges for probate of the will, receiving court authority to act on your behalf. He must take inventory of your estate and custody of the assets, review your financial records and administer your estate. This last could involve collecting income and other money due to the estate as well as paying any legacies, taxes and other costs in settling the estate.

Apart from your will, it is important that you discuss with your lawyer the need for executing a general power of attorney. This is a legal document appointing someone to act as your "attorney" – not a lawyer but someone who can do anything in law that you can do if you become sick or disabled, and unable to act. One example would be the need for action if you became incapacitated and were close to the end of your seventy-first year, when RRSPs must be cashed or converted into retirement income.

You can't take it with you. By taking a few simple steps, your wishes can be fulfilled with as little aggravation as possible to your beneficiaries. Seek qualified advice and take action today.

CHAPTER 40

Helping Your Favourite Charity

MANY PEOPLE IN THE SIXTY-plus age bracket want their families and a charity to inherit their money when they die. The trick is to structure your generosity so that as little of your wealth as possible falls into the hands of the taxman.

Anyone with a significant amount of money in guaranteed investment certificates or term deposits can link a charitable gift to an annuity. In doing this you give the charity a sum of money with which it buys an annuity from which you receive the income you need to live comfortably. Such a "charitable annuity" offers attractive tax and cash-flow advantages for both you and the registered charity of your choice.

Let's take the example of a man, sixty-five, who has $50,000 cash and requires an annual income of $5,000 from this capital. If he bought a life annuity with the money, he might receive about $5,500 a year. But he needs only $5,000 a year from the annuity, an income that would require the investment of only about $45,450.

Our sixty-five-year-old could give the $50,000 to the charity in return for a guaranteed lifetime income of $5,000 a year. (The charity will have to spend only $45,450 to buy an adequate life annuity.) Using the tables in Revenue Canada's IT-111R, we see this man has a life expectancy of 17.2 years. At an annual income of $5,000, the expected lifetime return on the annuity would be $86,000 (17.2 times $5,000).

Revenue Canada has set out guidelines for people who give money to registered charities in return for income payments through charitable annuities. In its circular IT-111R, available from district taxation offices, the department has indicated that if the lifetime income expected to be produced by an annuity is less than or equal to the amount of capital that you have given to a charity, the income you receive will be considered to be a return of capital and therefore tax-free.

In our example, because the lifetime return is greater than the amount given to the charity, the donor would not be entitled to a charitable tax credit. However, the income would be treated as if it were from a prescribed annuity. This means that the tax-free capital portion of each annuity payment would be based on the whole $50,000 gift. The donor benefits because the tax-free return-of-capital part of the $5,500 income received from the annuity each year would be greater than if he had bought the annuity directly from a life insurance company.

There are several ways to set up such a program, and they can be complex. However, with the help of your insurance agent or an annuity/RRIF broker, you can ease the most difficult problem facing charities today – securing a flow of cash to finance ongoing commitments.

For example, a sixty-five-year-old could buy a $45,450 life annuity himself and receive $5,500 a year from it. He could then donate the rest of his $50,000, the $4,550, to the charity. Going this route, he would receive the same income as he would in the situation described above, but more of each annuity payment would be taxable as interest income. However, he would have an immediate tax advantage from the charitable tax credit for his $4,550 donation. The charity is in the same position – it has received $4,550.

As a final choice, if the man wanted to protect himself in case his feelings about the charity change, he could use the full $50,000 to buy a life annuity. That would generate about $5,500 in annual income, leaving an extra $500 a year that could be donated to charity. He would receive an annual tax credit, and by retaining control of the income, he could vary or even stop annual gifts if circumstances change.

If the idea of funding a charity through an annuity is not appealing, you could consider donating part of your income from a GIC or term deposit. Though the interest would be taxable, you would receive a tax receipt for the amount your donate to the charity. This allows you to retain control of your capital. Then, at your death, your will could provide that the principal be paid to your estate for the benefit of a charity, or directly to the charity.

There are other ways you can provide more benefit to a charity and pay less tax. You might own land and a building that you would like to go to a charity. Let's say this property was bought for $100,000 and is now worth $1 million. There would be a $900,000 capital gain, on which the tax would be about $300,000. That would leave only $700,000 to give to the charity. It is unlikely you would be able to deduct the full $700,000. Charitable deductions are restricted to 20 percent of income a year and you can carry forward charitable gifts for only five years.

Rather than giving the charity the money from selling the property, you could just give the property to the charity. The Income Tax Act allows you to choose what the value of your donation will be – anywhere between the $100,000 original cost and the $1 million fair market value. If you estimate you can only use $500,000 over five years as a charitable contribution, you could give the property to the charity for $500,000 and get a charitable receipt for $500,000. You would only have to pay tax on $400,000, around $130,000 instead of $300,000. Similarly, an artist who wishes to donate a personal work to charity can determine what the value of the donation is. As a result, you won't lose out on deductions that you can't use fully because of the 20 percent of income and five-year carry-forward restrictions.

There are other strategies. For instance, there are special rules for Canadian cultural property. If you have a Canadian work of art that you would like to give to a museum or art gallery, you are not restricted to 20 percent of income a year as a deduction and you don't have to include the gain in income. If you donated a piece of Inuit art that you bought for $1,000 but is now worth $10,000, the gallery or museum would give you a special certificate designating that it is Canadian cultural property under the Canadian Import and Export Cultural Act and you would get a receipt for $10,000. But you would not have to include the $9,000 gain in your income.

Suppose you have a valuable coin or stamp collection that you would like to leave to a charity, but you want to keep it until your death. You can give the collection to the charity now, receive a charitable receipt, but retain a life interest in the collection. It would then go to the charity at your death. Talk about having your cake and eating it too!

Life insurance can also be used to benefit your favourite charity. Let's say you have an older policy that would not be needed by your family or estate. You could simply change the beneficiary to your favourite charity. This will not create any tax credit to you but on your death the charity will have the tax-free life insurance proceeds. If you want tax credits on death, designate your estate as the policy beneficiary and stipulate that the charity is to receive that amount in your will. There is one disadvantage to this method. The life insurance would be subject to probate fees since it is paid into your estate.

Some people purchase new life insurance policies on their lives for a charity. If the charity is the owner and beneficiary of the policy, you can receive a charitable tax receipt for the premiums paid.

If you have excess income during your retirement years, you can provide a much larger future gift than you might otherwise be able to through life insurance. If you want a charity to benefit from the wealth of your lifetime, seek qualified advice and consider one of the above alternatives.

CHAPTER 41

Snowbirds: Dealing With Uncle Sam

THOUGH MANY THOUSANDS of retired Canadians spend the winter in such sunshine states as Florida, Texas and Georgia, it is very difficult to immigrate to the United States – that is, to become a resident – unless you have close relatives who are U.S. citizens. Nevertheless, in many cases the United States and Canada will deem you to be a U.S. resident for income tax purposes even if you have not immigrated.

Anyone who spends a good deal of time in the United States should understand the tax implications as well as the financial impact the move will have on your health insurance, social security benefits and estate.

To begin, let's look at your health insurance. It is not a small sacrifice to give up Canada's provincially run health care insurance schemes to move to the U.S. Certainly one of the most significant advantages of remaining a Canadian resident is your continued eligibility for government health insurance.

If you are thinking of taking up U.S. residence, you should know that coverage formally ends three months after you leave Canada. If you allow this insurance to lapse, you should have private U.S. health insurance arranged, ready to kick in at that time.

If you intend to come back to Canada, however, the provincial health care systems will continue to protect you if you're outside your province for up to six months as long as you inform the government of your plan to remain a Canadian resident.

Even if you continue to be covered by Canadian government insurance, supplementary coverage from private insurance companies is necessary. Not only do older people tend to require more medical services, but your Canadian insurance only covers emergency medical services in the U.S. Even for approved services it usually pays only what that care would cost in Canada or, in some instances, only a portion of that. For example, the Ontario plan pays up to

$100 per day for hospital care. (U.S. medical bills are usually higher.) Also, you must be prepared to pay your U.S. medical bill immediately, send a claim to your provincial insurance plan and wait to be reimbursed.

Get a pamphlet from your provincial medical plan explaining what it covers outside the country. You'll find the names, addresses and phone numbers of the health care plans in the appendix, Where to Get More Information.

Moving to the United States will have less impact on your social security benefits. If you are entitled to Old Age Security and the CPP or QPP retirement benefit before you become a U.S. resident, it will be sent to you at your U.S. address just as it was sent to your home in Canada. Under the Canada-U.S. social security agreement, if you become a resident of the U.S. and subsequently begin to receive that country's social security, the time away from Canada will not decrease the amounts you would receive from the CPP.

Any Canada OAS, CPP or QPP benefit you receive will be 100 percent taxable in Canada. If you become a U.S. resident or are deemed to be a resident for income tax purposes, and receive these government pensions, they are only 50 percent taxable in the U.S. under the Canada-U.S. tax treaty. There is Canadian withholding tax on these benefits and you can't file a Canadian tax return to claim it back. You can, however, claim the withholding tax as a deduction against your U.S. tax.

Avoid being taxed twice on your RRSP

The income tax rules of Canada and the U.S. dovetail in more ways. If you move to the United States, will you continue to owe your tax allegiance to Revenue Canada or will it be the U.S. Internal Revenue Service? Generally, the Canadian income tax system taxes on residency. For the most part, Canada defines a resident as someone who voluntarily lives in the country for at least 183 days a year. The U.S. has it own definition that also stipulates at least 183 days of residence. In cases where a person would otherwise be deemed to be a resident of both countries for tax purposes, you can claim exemption from the taxes of one country through a "closer connection statement." Failure to make a statement is subject to penalties.

Let's consider registered retirement savings plans, a major source of retirement income for Canadians. To Revenue Canada, a RRSP is a tax shelter and the money is taxed only when it comes out. In the

U.S., however, the income earned in that RRSP will be taxed, although there are exceptions.

For Canadians who are U.S. residents, RRSP income must be reported to the U.S. – most of the time – but with no corresponding foreign tax credit. When you annuitize your RRSP, you are hit with Canadian tax on the interest that has accrued in the plan, but you don't get a credit for the U.S. taxes paid. In theory at least, you are taxed twice.

As mentioned, however, there are exceptions. The 1980 Canada-U.S. tax treaty, ratified in 1984, provided an election that gets around this problem. A U.S. resident or citizen can elect under Article XXIX(5) of the tax treaty not to have such income taxed until the money comes out. In this case, the income would be taxed by the U.S. and Canada concurrently but you would claim a foreign tax credit on your U.S. return.

Providing you make this election, there is no good reason if you are about to become a U.S. resident to annuitize your RRSPs before leaving. Of course, if economic conditions suggest that you do so (perhaps there are high interest rates at the time), you may choose to do so anyway.

To ensure that there is never any confusion over what is capital and what is income, some accountants advise their clients who are about to leave Canada and become U.S. residents, or residents for income tax purposes, to "capitalize" their RRSPs just before leaving. This means having the trustee of your RRSP roll it over, tax-free, into another RRSP. From the U.S. tax collector's viewpoint, whatever the value of your RRSP when this capitalization takes place is, it is all capital. U.S. taxation of the income begins at this point.

What happens if you decide to make cash withdrawals from your RRSP after becoming a U.S. resident? Under the Canada-U.S. tax treaty, 15 percent will be withheld by the financial institution administering your plan. An alternative available in limited circumstances is to withdraw from your RRSP amounts equal to your Canadian personal tax credits each year, approximately $7,000 in 1994. You would not be subject to tax in Canada on any of this income providing you file a Canadian tax return under Section 217 of the Income Tax Act. By making this election you will be taxed as a Canadian resident, thereby resulting in tax-free income up to your personal credits. There is however, one catch. New legislation states that this election will only be available if at least half of your taxable worldwide income is Canadian pension income.

Prior to collapsing an RRSP or making annual withdrawals, you should file form NR5 with Revenue Canada. This form is an undertaking that you will file a tax return and provides the RRSP plan trustee with authorization to give you the full withdrawal without withholding tax. (If there are Canadian taxes levied on your RRSP withdrawals, a foreign tax credit will be allowed on your U.S. income tax return.)

Reduce your taxes on rental income

There's another, similar election regarding rental income. It's something you might want to consider if you decide to rent out rather than sell your Canadian home. A non-resident of Canada who earns rental income in Canada is subject to 25 percent withholding tax on the gross income. The renter is required to deduct the 25 percent from the full rent and send it to Revenue Canada.

Instead, however, you can file a Canadian Section 216 tax return, giving you the right to pay tax on your net rental income, that is, the gross minus such expenses as mortgage interest, property taxes, maintenance and utilities. The tenant would then remit 25 percent of the net figure to Revenue Canada, and you would avoid overpaying on your withholding tax. Unlike the tax treatment of RRSP or RRIF income, you are not entitled to personal credits when you file a Canadian return to report rental income.

There are other tax strategies. When you emigrate from Canada, you are usually deemed to have disposed of most of your assets at fair market value. However, you don't have to dispose of certain assets that are considered taxable Canadian property, basically shares in a privately owned Canadian corporation, rental property, land and inventory. You can use these assets as collateral for any tax owing in future. If you eventually sell them, you will be subject to Canadian capital gains tax, but will be able to claim a foreign tax credit on your U.S. tax return.

If you sell your Canadian principal residence, of course, there will be no capital gains tax to pay because it is exempt. For other assets, the deemed disposition rule applies and you may have to pay income tax. However, if you have not used all of your lifetime $100,000 capital gains exemption, 1994 will be your last chance to use it.

Estate and gift taxes

There are two unpleasant and entirely unique tax animals in-
digenous to the United States called estate tax and gift tax, and
neither is covered under the Canada-U.S. tax treaty. You could be a
resident of Canada for income tax purposes but a resident of the
U.S. for gift and estate tax purposes.

Estate tax, or succession duty, is something Canada abandoned in
1971. In Canada, a person who dies is deemed to have disposed of
all assets at fair market value and, to the extent these assets do not
pass into the hands of the surviving spouse, capital gains tax is payable on the increase in value since 1971 or, if they were acquired
after that date, since they were acquired.

For U.S. residents and citizens, however, estate tax (or wealth
tax) comes into play instead. Under this tax, at death the fair market
value of all assets worldwide is determined, debt is deducted and
any amount over $600,000 is subject to the U.S. estate tax. As in
Canada, the exception is assets that pass into the hands of the surviving spouse. These don't become taxable until this person's death.

If you don't become a U.S. resident for tax purposes, but own assets in the United States, your estate could be hit with a hefty U.S.
estate tax bill because of the way the tax discriminates against foreigners. Representatives of Canada's Department of Finance and the
U.S. Treasury Department held extensive meetings on the problem,
but by mid-1994 there was still no resolution.

U.S. assets for estate tax purposes include not only real estate but
U.S. securities, such as stocks or bonds, and U.S. businesses owned
personally as partnerships or proprietorships. The tax hits virtually
all personally-owned U.S. assets except bank accounts, insurance
policies and art collections on loan to a museum. Estate taxes do
not apply on U.S. businesses that are Canadian corporations or are
owned by Canadian corporations. (Corporations don't pay estate tax.)

Before November 1988, foreigners holding U.S. assets faced
lighter U.S. estate taxes than Americans. Under a revised law that
went into effect at that time, everyone is subject to the same estate
tax rates, ranging from 18 percent on taxable estates worth $10,000
U.S. or less to 55 percent on amounts exceeding $3 million U.S. Un-
fortunately, there are differences on the application of the tax that
sharply tilt the tax scales against foreigners.

For one thing, Americans get an exemption on the first $600,000
U.S. of an estate, while non-resident non-citizens get only $60,000.

Differences in the calculation of net wealth (assets minus liabilities) for purposes of the tax can also disadvantage foreigners. In addition, if a non-resident non-citizen owns U.S. property jointly with a spouse, there is no provision for deferring the tax until the spouse dies, unless he or she is a U.S. citizen.

If you earn income in the U.S. and pay U.S. income tax, you generally get a credit on your Canadian tax return for the tax paid, as provided by the Canada-U.S. income tax treaty. There is no such Canadian credit for U.S. estate taxes. As a result, your estate could be hit when you die with U.S. estate tax and Canadian capital gains tax totalling as much as 80 percent, or possibly more, of the value of your U.S. assets.

There are ways for Canadians who own U.S. property but are not U.S. residents to ease the blow of estate taxes. However, every one of them has a drawback for every advantage.

Since the estate tax does not apply on corporately owned properties, you could incorporate a company that would own your U.S. house, condo or cottage.

Revenue Canada provides an administrative concession in this situation. Normally, if you have a corporation that owns personal-use property, the company must charge you with a taxable benefit for your use of the property. But if you have a Canadian corporation that buys a home or cottage in the U.S., and the only business of the corporation is to own it, Revenue Canada holds that the taxable benefit does not apply.

Now the problems. For one thing, many of the bylaws of U.S. condominium corporations bar corporations from owning the units. In Florida, most banks will not provide mortgages on homes owned by corporations.

If you decide that the single-purpose corporate route is best and already own your U.S. real estate, the property must be sold to your corporation at fair market value. That could mean you are hit with both U.S. and Canadian capital gains taxes that would have to be paid right away rather than the estate tax which is not payable until your death. In addition, a land transfer tax would be levied (known as stamping duties in the U.S.). Under the tax treaty, capital gains earned by Canadians in the U.S. are not taxable by the U.S. – except those on real estate. Moreover, while Canada taxes 75 percent of capital gains, the U.S. levy is on the full 100 percent.

The only relieving provision is that in Canada you would get a credit for the U.S. tax paid. You and/or your accountant will have to figure out whether it's better to pay income tax now or estate taxes in future.

You might consider buying a life insurance policy that would provide the money to pay your U.S. estate tax. This is a reasonable solution for many people, but it may be very expensive if you're getting on in years or your health is poor.

The estate tax exemption for foreigners is $60,000 a person. You could have a Florida condo worth $240,000 and escape estate taxes if you can share ownership, perhaps with your spouse and children, assuming your children provide their portion of the equity. Even if you ended up paying estate tax, the ownership-sharing strategy would reduce the tax bite. Of course, a family feud could create a major problem.

If this all sounds straightforward, be advised that most individual states also have their own estate taxes. You get a federal credit for the estate tax paid to the state. The estate tax makes will-planning for Canadians with U.S. assets especially troublesome. Plans you make to reduce your Canadian tax may only make your U.S. estate tax situation worse.

Finally, there's the U.S. gift tax. Uncle Sam taxes any gift to an individual that exceeds $10,000 U.S. a year and $100,000 over the lifetime of the recipient. The tax is on a graduated scale, from 18 percent to 49 percent.

Problems, problems. Just the same, a tax accountant and/or lawyer can help minimize them. If you remain a Canadian resident for tax purposes and own substantial U.S. assets, the key is to be aware of the pitfalls and put your financial advisors to work finding ways around them.

Taking Your Cod Liver Oil

IF YOU'RE OLD ENOUGH TO read this book on retirement planning, you're old enough to recall when mothers considered cod liver oil to be essential to good health.

As we wrap up *Retire Right*, we'd be happy if you'd view our advice in the same way your mother regarded cod liver oil: not great tasting, but good for you.

We have not tried to alarm you. But we hope we have alerted you to the necessity of long-range planning so you don't run the risk of outliving your income. We have described government pensions and employer pensions, and explained how RRSPs can make an essential difference to your retirement nest egg. We've spent much of this book going over annuities and RRIFs in their many variations so you can ensure that your RRSP generates the type of retirement income best suited to your needs.

Unless you're on the verge of retirement, the basics we've outlined in *Retire Right* will be of greatest interest. You can review the chapters describing the numerous options as you require more detail.

For now, you should pay attention to your employer's pension statements. Keep an eye on the annuity and RRIF tables in your newspaper to see how much retirement income your RRSPs would currently produce. And if it looks as if your retirement income is going to come up short, take corrective action: beef up your RRSPs.

Of course, the sooner you make your long-term assessment, the better. But it's never too late. Expanding RRSP contribution limits, along with your right to carry-forward unused contributions to future years, can do much to make up for years when you had too much current expense to worry about retirement.

And one final piece of advice: Despite all the planning in the world, you won't know for certain how well your income will be able to finance your retirement until you've actually retired.

We've seen people go a little crazy at retirement – buying a fancy new car, going on Caribbean vacations and generally spending like drunken sailors. Your needs will, in most cases, be less than during your working life. But we urge you to live modestly for the first six months of your retirement so you know for sure that you can live within reduced means if necessary. Then, every year or so, compare your spending with your income so you remain on track.

Remember that you may have a long retirement. We certainly hope you will. All the more reason to ensure you have the money to enjoy it thoroughly – and you will if you retire right.

Where to Get More Information

WE HOPE *RETIRE RIGHT* HAS answered many of your questions on retirement income. However, we realize we've probably raised a few as well.

You might wonder, for instance, whether you're eligible for federal or provincial income supplements. Or if you immigrated to Canada, do you qualify for a pension from your country of origin? Perhaps you'd like to ask the relevant regulatory authority about your employer pension or a life insurance product.

Maybe you'd like to read more about financial subjects, such as RRSPs, life insurance and investing, which we discussed only in relation to annuities and RRIFs.

The following list of information sources and recommended reading will help. To find an annuity/RRIF broker, look under "Annuities" in the yellow pages of your telephone directory.

Financial Institutions

Banks

Canadian Bankers' Association
P.O. Box 348, 2 First Canadian Place
Toronto, Ontario M5X 1E1

Life insurance

The Canadian Life and Health Insurance Association offers free booklets and pamphlets, not only on life and disability insurance, but also on estate planning, retirement planning and other aspects of personal finance. The address is:

Communications Department
Canadian Life and Health Insurance Association
1 Queen St. E., Suite 1700
Toronto, Ontario M5C 2X9

You can also call the association's information service free of charge from anywhere in Canada by dialling 1-800-268-8099 between 9 a.m. to 5 p.m. (Eastern time) on business days.

Trust companies
Trust Companies Association of Canada
50 O'Connor St., Suite 720
Ottawa, Ontario K1P 6L2

Canadian and Foreign Pensions
Canada Pension Plan, Old Age Security, Guaranteed Income Supplement, and Spouse's Allowance
Look for Income Security Programs under "H" (for Human Resources Development Canada) in the blue Government of Canada pages at the back of your white pages telephone directory.

British pensions
British Pensioners' Association (Canada)
605 Royal York Rd., Suite 202
Etobicoke, Ontario M8Y 4G5
Department of Health and Social Security
Longbenton, Newcastle-on-Tyne
England NE98 1YX

Italian pensions
INAS-Canada
1263 Wilson Ave.
Downsview, Ontario M3M 3G2

U.S. Social Security
United States Embassy
100 Wellington St.
Ottawa, Ontario K1P 5T1
Phone (613) 238-5335

Regulatory Authorities
The overall regulator in Ottawa is the Superintendent of Financial Institutions, with authority over the banks, federally regulated trust companies, loan and investment companies, and pensions governed by the federal Pension Benefits Standards Act (including those in the Yukon and Northwest Territories). It also has jurisdiction over

federally incorporated life insurance companies and federally incorporated property and casualty companies. The address is:

Office of the Superintendent of Financial Institutions
255 Albert St., 16th floor
Ottawa, Ontario K1A 0H2

If you have questions about the products of provincially incorporated life insurance companies, or if your pension is subject to provincial authority, ask the appropriate provincial regulator.

Provincial and Territorial Life Insurance Regulators

Alberta
Superintendent of Insurance
Ministry of Consumer and Corporate Affairs
19th floor, 10025 Jasper Ave.
Edmonton, Alberta T5J 3Z5

British Columbia
Superintendent of Insurance
Ministry of Finance and Corporate Relations
1900 1050 W. Pender St.
Vancouver, British Columbia V6E 3S7

Manitoba
Superintendent of Insurance
Ministry of Consumer and Corporate Affairs
Woodsworth Building, Room 1142
405 Broadway Ave.
Winnipeg, Manitoba R3C 3L6

New Brunswick
Superintendent of Insurance
Department of Insurance
Room 477, Centennial Building
P.O. Box 6000
Fredericton, New Brunswick E3B 5H1

Newfoundland
Superintendent of Insurance
Department of Justice
2nd floor, 100 Elizabeth Avenue
P.O. Box 8700
St. John's, Newfoundland A1B 4J6

Northwest Territories
Superintendent of Insurance
Ministry of Justice, Consumer and Corporate Affairs
Box 1320
Yellowknife, Northwest Territories X1A 2L9

Nova Scotia
Superintendent of Insurance
40 Alderney Drive
P.O. Box 815
Dartmouth, Nova Scotia B2Y 3Z3

Ontario
Superintendent of Insurance
Ontario Insurance Commission
16th Floor, 5160 Yonge St.
Box 85
North York, Ontario M2N 6L9

Prince Edward Island
Superintendent of Insurance
Ministry of Justice
Shaw Building, 73 Rochford St.
P.O. Box 2000
Charlottetown, Prince Edward Island C1A 7N8

Quebec
Superintendent of Insurance
800 Place d'Youville, Suite 801
Quebec City, Quebec G1R 4Y5

Saskatchewan
Superintendent of Insurance
1871 Smith St.
Regina, Saskatchewan S4P 3V7

Yukon Territory
Superintendent of Insurance
Ministry of Consumer and Corporate Affairs
3rd floor, 2134 Second Avenue
P.O. Box 2703
Whitehorse, Yukon Y1A 2C6

Provincial Pension Regulators

Alberta
Superintendent of Pensions
Alberta Labour Employment Pensions Branch
10808 99th Avenue, Room 401
Edmonton, Alberta T5K 0G5

British Columbia
Superannuation Commissioner
Government of British Columbia
548 Michigan St.
Victoria, British Columbia V8V 4R5

Manitoba
Superintendent of Pensions
Pension Commission of Manitoba
401 York Ave., Suite 1004
Winnipeg, Manitoba R3C 0P8

New Brunswick
Superintendent of Pensions
Dept. of Advanced Education & Labour
Pensions Branch
P.O. Box 6000
Fredericton, New Brunswick E3B 5H1

Newfoundland
Superintendent of Pensions
Ministry of Finance
P.O. Box 8700
St. John's, Newfoundland A1B 4J6

Nova Scotia
Superintendent of Pensions
Department of Finance
P.O. Box 187
Halifax, Nova Scotia B3J 2N3

Ontario
Superintendent of Pensions
Pension Commission of Ontario
101 Bloor St. W., 9th floor
Toronto, Ontario M7A 2K2

Prince Edward Island
Director
Economics, Statistics and Fiscal Analysis Division
Department of Finance
P.O. Box 2000
Charlottetown, Prince Edward Island C1A 7N8

Quebec
Quebec Pension Plan
2635 Boul. Hochelaga, 5th floor
Ste-Foy, Quebec G1V 4T3
The QPP is both the regulator of employer pensions in the province
and the Quebec equivalent of the CPP.

Saskatchewan
Superintendent of Pensions
Department of Labour
1870 Albert St.
Regina, Saskatchewan S4P 3V7

Provincial/Territorial Pension Supplements
Alberta
Alberta Assured Income Plan
Ministry of Social Services
12th floor, Centre West
10035, 108th St.
Edmonton, Alberta T5J 3E1

British Columbia
Guaranteed Available Income for the Needy (GAIN)
Ministry of Social Services and Housing
P.O. Box 2500
Victoria, British Columbia V8W 3A1

Manitoba
"Fifty-five plus"
Income Supplement Programs Office
Ministry of Employment Services and Economic Security
Box 5000, 316 4th Ave.
Carberry, Manitoba

Northwest Territories
N.W.T. Senior Citizens' Supplementary Benefits
Ministry of Social Services
P.O. Box 1320
Yellowknife, Northwest Territories X1A 2L9

Nova Scotia
Seniors' Assistance Program
Department of Community Services
P.O. Box 1661
Halifax, Nova Scotia B3J 3A2

Ontario
Guaranteed Annual Income System (GAINS)
Ministry of Revenue
33 King St. W.
Oshawa, Ontario L1H 8H8

Quebec Pension Plan
2635 Boul. Hochelaga, 5th floor
Ste-Foy, Quebec G1V 4T3

Saskatchewan
Saskatchewan Income Plan
Saskatchewan Seniors' Secretariat
2151 Scarth St.
Regina, Saskatchewan S4P 3Z3

Yukon Territory
Yukon Seniors' Income Supplement
Ministry of Health and Social Services
Dept. H4
P.O. Box 2703
Whitehorse, Yukon Territory Y1A 2C6

U.S. Sources of Information
United States Embassy
100 Wellington St.
Ottawa, Ontario K1P 5T1
Direct your questions on U.S. tax to Joe Hook, tax attaché; questions on U.S. immigration to Pamela Carrozza, immigration attaché.

Provincial Medicare Offices

Alberta
Health Care Insurance
10025 Jasper Ave.
Edmonton, Alberta T5J 2N3

British Columbia
Medical Services Plan
P.O. Box 1600
Victoria, British Columbia V8W 2X9

Manitoba
Manitoba Health Services Commission
P.O. Box 925
599 Empress St.
Winnipeg, Manitoba R3C 2T6

New Brunswick
Department of Health and Community Services
Carleton Place, P.O. Box 5100
Fredericton, New Brunswick E3B 5G8

Newfoundland
Newfoundland Medical Care Commission
P.O. Box 200, Stn. A
St. John's, Newfoundland A1C 5J3

Northwest Territories
Health Insurance Administration
Department of Health
P.O. Box 1320
Yellowknife, Northwest Territories X1A 2L9

Nova Scotia
Insured Professional Services Division
Department of Health
Box 488
Halifax, Nova Scotia B3J 2R8

Ontario
Ontario Health Insurance Plan
49 Place d'Armes
Kingston, Ontario K7L 5J3

Prince Edward Island
Hospital and Health Services Commission
P.O. Box 3000
Montague, Prince Edward Island C0A 1R0

Quebec
Régie de l'assurance maladie du Quebec
Case postale 6600
Quebec City, Quebec G1K 7T3

Saskatchewan
Saskatchewan Health
3475 Albert St.
Regina, Saskatchewan S4S 6X6

Yukon
Department of Health and Social Services
P.O. Box 2703
Whitehorse, Yukon Y1A 2C6

Recommended Reading

For information on personal finance issues, we recommend the other books in the Financial Times Personal Finance Library, co-published by Penguin Books Canada. They include:

Investment Strategies: How to Create Your Own and Make It Work For You by Seymour Friedland and Steven G. Kelman

The Money Companion: How to Manage Your Money and Achieve Financial Freedom by Elaine Wyatt

RRSPs 1995: Everything You Need to Know to Make the Right Choices by Steven G. Kelman

Understanding Mutual Funds: Your No-Nonsense Everyday Guide by Steven G. Kelman

The Gold Book: The Complete Investment Guide to Precious Metals by Pierre Lassonde

Bulls And Bears: Winning in the Stock Market in Good Times and Bad by Hugh Anderson

Money For Rent: A Guide to Earning Top Interest on Your Savings by Hugh Anderson

Insure Sensibly: A Guide to Life and Disability Insurance by James Bullock and George Brett

We also recommend:

How To Reduce The Tax You Pay by accountants at Deloitte & Touche, Key Porter Books Ltd.

Whose Money Is It Anyway? by Ann Finlayson, Penguin Books Canada Ltd.

Your Pension: The Complete Guide To Pension Planning In Canada by Patrick Longhurst and Rose Marie Earle, Doubleday Canada Ltd.

Risk Is A Four Letter Word by George Hartman, Hartman & Company

Index